Entertainment Dire

BRIGHTON
TRAVEL GUIDE
2015

SHOPS, RESTAURANTS, ATTRACTIONS & NIGHTLIFE

The Most Positively Reviewed and Recommended by Locals and Travelers

EGP Editorial

BRIGHTON
TRAVEL GUIDE
2015

SHOPS, RESTAURANTS, ATTRACTIONS & NIGHTLIFE

BRIGHTON TRAVEL GUIDE 2015
Shops, Restaurants, Attractions & Nightlife

Web: http://www.EGPGuides.com/

ISBN-13: 978-1505334579
ISBN-10: 1505334578

EGP
Editorial

INDEX

SHOPS

Top 500 Shops - 9

RESTAURANTS

Top 500 Restaurants - 49

ATTRACTIONS

Top 450 Attractions - 87

NIGHTLIFE

Top 450 Nightlife Spots - 119

BRIGHTON TRAVEL GUIDE 2015

Shops, Restaurants, Attractions & Nightlife

This directory is dedicated to Brighton Business Owners and Managers who provide the experience that the locals and tourists enjoy. Thanks you very much for all that you do and thank for being the "People Choice".

Thanks to everyone that posts their reviews online and the amazing reviews sites that make our life easier.

The places listed in this book are the most positively reviewed and recommended by locals and travelers from around the world.

Thank you for your time and enjoy the directory that is designed with locals and tourist in mind!

TOP 500 SHOPS

Recommended by Locals & Trevelers

(From #1 to #500)

#1
Resident
Category: Music & DVDs
Average price: Inexpensive
Address: 28 Kensington Gardens
Brighton BN1 4AL, UK
Phone: +44 1273 606312

#2
Get Cutie
Category: Women's Clothing
Average price: Modest
Address: 33 Kensington Gardens
Brighton BN1 4AL, UK
Phone: +44 1273 688575

#3
Bert's Homestore
Category: Kitchen & Bath, Home Decor
Average price: Modest
Address: 155-156 Western Road
Brighton BN1 2DA, UK
Phone: +44 1273 774212

#4
Dave's Comics
Category: Comic Books
Average price: Modest
Address: 5 Sydney Street
Brighton BN1 4EN, UK
Phone: +44 1273 691012

#5
Brighton Flea Market
Category: Antiques, Furniture Store
Average price: Modest
Address: 31a Upper Street
Brighton BN2 1JN, UK
Phone: +44 1273 624006

#6
Colin Page Antiquarian Books
Category: Bookstore
Average price: Modest
Address: 36 Duke Street
Brighton BN1 1AG, UK
Phone: +44 1273 325954

#7
Steamer Trading Cook Shop
Category: Kitchen & Bath, Home Decor
Average price: Expensive
Address: 35 Ship Street
Brighton BN1 1AB, UK
Phone: +44 1273 227705

#8
Jump The Gun
Category: Men's Clothing
Average price: Expensive
Address: 36 Gardner Street
Brighton BN1 1UN, UK
Phone: +44 1273 626333

#9
Modelzone
Category: Hobby Shop
Average price: Expensive
Address: 37 West Street
Brighton BN1 2RE, UK
Phone: +44 1273 326790

#10
Brighton Bead Shop
Category: Hobby Shop, Jewelry, Arts & Crafts
Average price: Expensive
Address: 21 Sydney Street
Brighton BN1 4EN, UK
Phone: +44 1273 675077

#11
Taylor's
Category: Tobacco Shop
Average price: Modest
Address: 19 Bond Street
Brighton BN1 1RD, UK
Phone: +44 1273 606110

#12
Artrepublic Art Gallery
Category: Art Gallery, Arts & Crafts
Average price: Modest
Address: 13 Bond Street
Brighton BN1 1RD, UK
Phone: +44 1273 724829

#13
Blackout
Category: Flowers & Gifts
Average price: Modest
Address: 53 Kensington Place
Brighton BN1 4EJ, UK
Phone: +44 1273 671741

#14
Brighton Museum & Art Gallery
Category: Museum, Art Gallery
Average price: Inexpensive
Address: 4-5 Pavilion Buildings
Brighton BN1 1EE, UK
Phone: +44 30 0029 0900

#15
Ditto Fabrics
Category: Fabric Store
Average price: Modest
Address: 21 Kensington Gardens
Brighton BN1 4AL, UK
Phone: +44 1273 603771

#16
Malarkey
Category: Cards & Stationery
Average price: Expensive
Address: 34 Bond Street
Brighton BN1 1RD, UK
Phone: +44 1273 722339

#17
Castor + Pollux
Category: Bookstore, Art Gallery
Average price: Expensive
Address: 164-166 Kings Road Arches
Brighton BN1 1NB, UK
Phone: +44 1273 773776

#18
Mad Hatters
Category: Accessories
Average price: Modest
Address: 89 Trafalgar Street
Brighton BN1 4ER, UK
Phone: +44 1273 688488

#19
Adaptatrap Musical Instruments
Category: Musical Instruments
Average price: Modest
Address: 26 Trafalgar Street
Brighton BN1 4ED, UK
Phone: +44 1273 672722

#20
Swift Sports
Category: Sporting Goods
Average price: Modest
Address: 39 Grand Parade
Brighton BN2 9QA, UK
Phone: +44 1273 605625

#21
Acacia Designs
Category: Arts & Crafts, Furniture Store
Average price: Expensive
Address: 19-21 Elder Place
Brighton BN1 4GF, UK
Phone: +44 7770 793388

#22
The Sussex Beacon
Category: Thrift Store
Average price: Inexpensive
Address: 130 St James's Street
Brighton BN2 1TH, UK
Phone: +44 1273 682992

#23
Fabric Land
Category: Fabric Store
Average price: Inexpensive
Address: 76 Western Rd
Brighton BN1 2HA, UK
Phone: +44 1273 822257

#24
Revamp
Category: Costumes
Average price: Modest
Address: 11 Sydney Street
Brighton BN1 4EN, UK
Phone: +44 1273 623288

#25
Junkfunk
Category: Men's Clothing, Arts & Crafts
Average price: Modest
Address: 27 Gloucester Road
Brighton BN1 4AQ, UK
Phone: +44 1273 680555

#26
Wax Factor
Category: Bookstore
Average price: Expensive
Address: 24 Trafalgar Street
Brighton BN1 4ED, UK
Phone: +44 1273 673744

#27
Beyond Retro
Category: Vintage & Consignment
Average price: Modest
Address: 42 Vine Street
Brighton BN1 4AG, UK
Phone: +44 1273 671937

#28
Jubilee Library
Category: Library, Books, Music & Video
Average price: Inexpensive
Address: Jubilee Street
Brighton BN1 1GE, UK
Phone: +44 1273 290800

#29
Johns Camping International
Category: Outdoor Gear
Average price: Modest
Address: 89 London Road
Brighton BN1 4JF, UK
Phone: +44 1273 684000

#30
Purple-Heart.com
Category: Bakery, Party Supplies, Cards & Stationery
Average price: Modest
Address: 22 Gardner Street
Brighton BN1 1UP, UK
Phone: +44 1273 696935

#31
Shabitat
Category: Furniture Store, Thrift Store
Average price: Inexpensive
Address: Lewes Road
Brighton BN2 4AE, UK
Phone: +44 1273 684425

#32
Lavender / Room
Category: Women's Clothing
Average price: Expensive
Address: 16 Bond Street
Brighton BN1 1RD, UK
Phone: +44 1273 220380

#33
Lush
Category: Cosmetics & Beauty Supply
Average price: Modest
Address: 41 East Street
Brighton BN1 1HL, UK
Phone: +44 1273 774700

#34
Fabrica
Category: Art Gallery, Museum
Average price: Inexpensive
Address: Ship Street
Brighton BN1 1AB, UK
Phone: +44 1273 778646

#35
C & H Fabrics
Category: Fabric Store
Average price: Expensive
Address: 179-180 Western Road
Brighton BN1 2BA, UK
Phone: +44 1273 321959

#36
O2
Category: Mobile Phones
Average price: Modest
Address: 203-205 Western Road
Brighton BN1 2BA, UK
Phone: +44 1273 770112

#37
New Fabric Fair
Category: Fabric Store
Average price: Inexpensive
Address: 51 Gardner Street
Brighton BN1 1UN, UK
Phone: +44 1273 605512

#38
Greenwich Village
Category: Women's Clothing, Accessories
Average price: Expensive
Address: 17 Bond Street
Brighton BN1 1RD, UK
Phone: +44 1273 695451

#39
Richer Sounds
Category: Electronics
Average price: Modest
Address: 54 London Road
Brighton BN1 4JE, UK
Phone: +44 1273 673333

#40
Pussy
Category: Home & Garden
Average price: Expensive
Address: 3a Kensington Gardens
Brighton BN1 4AL, UK
Phone: +44 1273 604861

#41
Big Ears
Category: Jewelry, Watches
Average price: Modest
Address: 143a North Street
Brighton BN1 1RE, UK
Phone: +44 1273 326292

#42
Mamissima
Category: Maternity Wear
Average price: Modest
Address: 82 North Road
Brighton BN1 1YD, UK
Phone: +44 1273 626676

#43
Surf & Ski Sports
Category: Outdoor Gear
Average price: Modest
Address: 1-2 Regent Street
Brighton BN1 1UL, UK
Phone: +44 1273 673192

#44
Boots
Category: Drugstore, Cosmetics & Beauty Supply, Eyewear & Opticians
Average price: Modest
Address: 129 North Street
Brighton BN1 2BE, UK
Phone: +44 1273 207461

#45
Jog Shop
Category: Sporting Goods
Average price: Modest
Address: 39b George Street
Brighton BN2 1RJ, UK
Phone: +44 1273 675717

#46
Size?
Category: Sporting Goods, Shoe Store
Average price: Modest
Address: 32-36 North Street
Brighton BN1 1EB, UK
Phone: +44 1273 728113

#47
Vintage Magazine Co
Category: Books, Mags, Music & Video, Accessories, Hobby Shop
Average price: Modest
Address: 37 Kensington Gardens
Brighton BN1 4, UK
Phone: +44 1273 671812

#48
Lego Store
Category: Toy Store
Average price: Expensive
Address: Churchill Square
Brighton BN1 2TA, UK
Phone: +44 1273 772670

#49
Living At Fiveways
Category: Flowers & Gifts, Jewelry
Average price: Modest
Address: 296 Ditchling Rd
Brighton BN1 6JG, UK
Phone: +44 1273 563344

#50
Painting Pottery Cafe
Category: Art Schools, Hobby Shop
Average price: Inexpensive
Address: 31 North Road
Brighton BN1 1YB, UK
Phone: +44 1273 628952

#51
HMV
Category: Music & DVDs
Average price: Modest
Address: 61-62 Western Rd
Brighton BN1 2HA, UK
Phone: +44 1273 747221

#52
99p Stores
Category: Home & Garden
Average price: Inexpensive
Address: 143 N St
Brighton BN1 1RG, UK
Phone: +44 1273 778633

#53
Bert's Homestore
Category: Kitchen & Bath
Average price: Modest
Address: 33 George St
Brighton BN3 3YB, UK
Phone: +44 1273 732770

#54
Record Album
Category: Music & DVDs
Average price: Modest
Address: 8 Terminus Road
Brighton BN1 3PD, UK
Phone: +44 1273 323853

#55
Robert Dyas
Category: Hardware Store, Electronics
Average price: Inexpensive
Address: 74 Western Road
Brighton BN1 2HA, UK
Phone: +44 1273 324881

#56
Sandpiper
Category: Bookstore
Average price: Modest
Address: 34 Kensington Gardens
Brighton BN1 4AL, UK
Phone: +44 1273 605422

#57
Fun Learning
Category: Toy Store
Average price: Modest
Address: 5 North Street
Brighton BN1 1EB, UK
Phone: +44 1273 735134

#58
England At Home Furniture
Category: Furniture Store, Home Decor
Average price: Expensive
Address: 22b Ship St
Brighton BN1 1AD, UK
Phone: +44 1273 205544

#59
Espressa
Category: Videos & Video Game Rental
Average price: Inexpensive
Address: 86 Lewes Road
Brighton BN2 3HZ, UK
Phone: +44 1273 687770

#60
Zoingimage
Category: Arts & Crafts, Photography
Average price: Modest
Address: 1 Sydney Street
Brighton BN1 4EN, UK
Phone: +44 1273 686568

#61
Gresham Blake
Category: Sewing & Alterations,
Men's Clothing, Women's Clothing
Average price: Expensive
Address: 20 Bond Street
Brighton BN1 1RD, UK
Phone: +44 1273 609587

#62
Maplin Electronics
Category: Electronics,
Musical Instruments, Computers
Average price: Modest
Address: 65-66 London Road
Brighton BN1 4JE, UK
Phone: +44 1273 620930

#63
Debenhams
Category: Department Store
Average price: Modest
Address: Churchill Square Shopping Ctr
Brighton BN1 2TE, UK
Phone: +44 844 561 6161

#64
England At Home
Category: Home & Garden
Average price: Modest
Address: 59 Ship St
Brighton BN1 1AE, UK
Phone: +44 1273 738270

#65
Pure South
Category: Arts & Crafts
Average price: Modest
Address: 6 Meeting House Lane
Brighton BN1 1HB, UK
Phone: +44 1273 321718

#66
Gill's Home and Garden
Category: Hardware Store
Average price: Modest
Address: 97 Western Road
Brighton BN3 1FA, UK
Phone: +44 1273 772602

#67
Brighton Marina
Category: Boating, Leisure Center
Average price: Expensive
Address: Brighton Marina Estate Company,
Brighton BN1 4EN, UK
Phone: +44 1273 628627

#68
Clarkes Stationers
Category: Cards & Stationery, Printing
Services, Arts & Entertainment
Average price: Modest
Address: 11 Bond Street
Brighton BN1 1RD, UK
Phone: +44 1273 728811

#69
Clock Tower Cameras
Category: Photography Store,
Electronics Repair
Average price: Modest
Address: 32 Church Street
Brighton BN1 1RL, UK
Phone: +44 1273 706010

#70
Smokers Heaven
Category: Tobacco Shop
Average price: Modest
Address: 10 Queens Road
Brighton BN1 3WA, UK
Phone: +44 1273 321716

#71
Brighton & Hove Albion F C Club Shop
Category: Sporting Goods, Soccer
Average price: Expensive
Address: 6 Queens Road
Brighton BN1 3WB, UK
Phone: +44 1273 776969

#72
Evans Cycles
Category: Bikes
Average price: Expensive
Address: 4 Air St
Brighton BN1 3FB, UK
Phone: +44 1273 772357

#73
The Guitar, Amp & Keyboard Centre
Category: Musical Instruments
Average price: Modest
Address: 77-81 N Road
Brighton BN1 1YD, UK
Phone: +44 1273 672977

#74
Gunns Flowers
Category: Florist
Average price: Modest
Address: 13-14 Sydney Street
Brighton BN1 4EN, UK
Phone: +44 1273 683038

#75
Swag
Category: Antiques, Home Decor
Average price: Expensive
Address: 91 Trafalgar Street
Brighton BN1 4ER, UK
Phone: +44 1273 688504

#76
The Lollipop Shoppe
Category: Furniture Store
Average price: Expensive
Address: 5 Prince Albert Street
Brighton BN1 1HE, UK
Phone: +44 1273 770324

#77
Pretty Eccentric
Category: Furniture Store
Average price: Expensive
Address: 26 N Street
Brighton BN1 1EB, UK
Phone: +44 7870 607925

#78
University of Brighton Gallery
Category: Art Gallery
Average price: Inexpensive
Address: Grand Parade
Brighton BN2 0JY, UK
Phone: +44 1273 643012

#79
The Vault
Category: Photography Store
Average price: Expensive
Address: 1 Dorset Place
Brighton BN2 1ST, UK
Phone: +44 1273 670667

#80
Oddballs
Category: Sporting Goods, Hobby Shop
Average price: Modest
Address: 24 Kensington Gardens
Brighton BN1 4AL, UK
Phone: +44 1273 696068

#81
Mama San
Category: Women's Clothing, Accessories
Average price: Modest
Address: 102 Gloucester Road
Brighton BN1 4AP, UK
Phone: +44 1273 623388

#82
Wolf and Gypsy
Category: Vintage & Consignment, Accessories, Women's Clothing
Average price: Expensive
Address: 30 Sydney Street
Brighton BN1 4EP, UK
Phone: +44 1273 671797

#83
Cult Hero
Category: Music & DVDs, Bookstore
Average price: Modest
Address: 25 North Street
Brighton BN1 1EB, UK
Phone: +44 1273 771959

#84
Across The Tracks
Category: Music & DVDs
Average price: Inexpensive
Address: 110 Gloucester Road
Brighton BN1 4AF, UK
Phone: +44 1273 677906

#85
Baker Street Bikes
Category: Bikes
Average price: Modest
Address: 7-8 York Place
Brighton BN1 4GU, UK
Phone: +44 1273 675754

#86
Yashar Bish
Category: Home Decor, Furniture Store
Average price: Modest
Address: 96 Gloucester Road
Brighton BN1 4AP, UK
Phone: +44 1273 671900

#87
Ink-d
Category: Art Gallery
Average price: Expensive
Address: 96 North Road
Brighton BN1 1YE, UK
Phone: +44 1273 645299

#88
TK Maxx
Category: Discount Store
Average price: Inexpensive
Address: 36-37 North St
Brighton BN1 1EB, UK
Phone: +44 1273 727483

#89
Cath Kidston
Category: Fashion, Home & Garden
Average price: Expensive
Address: 31-32a East St
Brighton BN1 1HL, UK
Phone: +44 1273 227420

#90
Ginger Lily Florists
Category: Florist
Average price: Modest
Address: 93 Preston Drove
Brighton BN1 6LD, UK
Phone: +44 1273 504904

#91
Parker Bathrooms & Kitchens
Category: Kitchen & Bath
Average price: Expensive
Address: 64-80 Dyke Road
Brighton BN1 3JD, UK
Phone: +44 1273 329829

#92
Wood Store
Category: Hardware Store, Furniture Store, Home Decor
Average price: Modest
Address: Circus Street
Brighton BN2 9QF, UK
Phone: +44 1273 570500

#93
Velvet
Category: Flowers & Gifts, Home Decor, Furniture Store
Average price: Modest
Address: 27 Bond St
Brighton BN1 1RD, UK
Phone: +44 1273 326322

#94
Chris Hawkins Jewellery
Category: Jewelry
Average price: Expensive
Address: 79 Beaconsfield Road
Brighton BN1 6, UK
Phone: +44 1273 554632

#95
Cocoon
Category: Fabric Store
Average price: Expensive
Address: 10 George Street
Brighton BN3 3YA, UK
Phone: +44 1273 776176

#96
Robert Dyas
Category: Appliances, Electronics, Hardware Store
Average price: Modest
Address: 96 George Street
Brighton BN3 3YE, UK
Phone: +44 1273 220763

#97
Ju-Ju
Category: Women's Clothing, Men's Clothing, Accessories
Average price: Modest
Address: 24 Gloucester Rd
Brighton BN1 4AQ, UK
Phone: +44 1273 673161

#98
Tinkers
Category: Hardware Store
Average price: Modest
Address: 104 Dyke Road
Brighton BN1 3JD, UK
Phone: +44 1273 729523

#99
Rainbow Books
Category: Bookstore
Average price: Inexpensive
Address: 28 Trafalgar St
Brighton BN1 4ED, UK
Phone: +44 1273 605101

#100
Snoopers Paradise
Category: Antiques, Home & Garden
Average price: Modest
Address: 7-8 Kensington Gardens
Brighton BN1 4AL, UK
Phone: +44 1273 602558

#101
Timeslip
Category: Music & DVDs
Average price: Modest
Address: 90 Trafalgar St
Brighton BN1 4ER, UK
Phone: +44 1273 609006

#102
Offspring
Category: Shoe Store
Average price: Modest
Address: 25 Duke Street
Brighton BN1 1AG, UK
Phone: +44 1273 329363

#103
North Laine Antique & Flea Market
Category: Antiques
Average price: Modest
Address: 5-5a Upper Gardner St
Brighton BN1 1, UK
Phone: +44 1273 600894

#104
Lulu Rose
Category: Women's Clothing
Average price: Modest
Address: 27 Kensington Gardens
Brighton BN1 4AL, UK
Phone: +44 1273 697944

#105
Gunns
Category: Florist
Average price: Modest
Address: 6 Castle Square
Brighton BN1 1EG, UK
Phone: +44 1273 207490

#106
Jeremy Hoye Jewellers
Category: Jewelry
Average price: Modest
Address: 22A Ship Street
Brighton BN1 1AD, UK
Phone: +44 1273 777207

#107
In My Room
Category: Furniture Store, Antiques
Average price: Expensive
Address: 35 Gloucester Road
Brighton BN1 4AQ, UK
Phone: +44 1273 675506

#108
The Futon Co
Category: Furniture Store
Average price: Expensive
Address: 51 Preston St
Brighton BN1 2HP, UK
Phone: +44 1273 723810

#109
io Gallery
Category: Art Gallery, Arts & Crafts, Flowers & Gifts
Average price: Modest
Address: 39 Sydney Street
Brighton BN1 4EP, UK
Phone: +44 1273 671212

#110
Ananda
Category: Furniture Store, Arts & Crafts
Average price: Expensive
Address: 24 Bond Street
Brighton BN1 1RD, UK
Phone: +44 1273 725307

#111
Jaba Yard Mens Ladies Clothing
Category: Fashion
Average price: Modest
Address: 18 Bond Street
Brighton BN1 1RD, UK
Phone: +44 1273 623244

#112
Route One
Category: Sports Wear, Men's Clothing
Average price: Modest
Address: 3 Bond St
Brighton BN1 1RD, UK
Phone: +44 1273 323633

#113
Lulu & Hitch
Category: Gift Shop
Average price: Modest
Address: 44 Church Rd
Brighton BN3 2FN, UK
Phone: +44 1273 773758

#114
American Apparel
Category: Women's Clothing, Men's Clothing
Average price: Modest
Address: 18 North Street
Brighton BN1 1EB, UK
Phone: +44 1273 730509

#115
Fair
Category: Children's Clothing, Women's Clothing
Average price: Modest
Address: 21 Queens Road
Brighton BN1 3XA, UK
Phone: +44 1273 723215

#116
Mumbles Emporium
Category: Furniture Store
Average price: Expensive
Address: 25 Gloucester Road
Brighton BN1 4AQ, UK
Phone: +44 7861 390084

#117
Gap Kids
Category: Children's Clothing
Average price: Modest
Address: 16-19 E Street
Brighton BN1 1HP, UK
Phone: +44 1273 739683

#118
Gaff
Category: Home Decor
Average price: Modest
Address: 66 Trafalgar Street
Brighton BN1 4EB, UK
Phone: +44 1273 819202

#119
Rin-Tin-Tin
Category: Antiques
Average price: Modest
Address: 34 North Road
Brighton BN1 1YB, UK
Phone: +44 1273 672424

#120
Caz Systems
Category: Furniture Store, Appliances
Average price: Expensive
Address: 18-19 Church St
Brighton BN1 1RB, UK
Phone: +44 1273 326471

#121
Yummies
Category: Children's Clothing
Average price: Modest
Address: 15 Bond Street
Brighton BN1 1RD, UK
Phone: +44 1273 738733

#122
Sole Trader
Category: Shoe Store
Average price: Modest
Address: Unit 31 Churchill Sq
Brighton BN1 2TD, UK
Phone: +44 1273 204822

#123
Primark
Category: Women's Clothing, Men's Clothing
Average price: Inexpensive
Address: 188-191 Western Road
Brighton BN1 2BA, UK
Phone: +44 1273 205211

#124
RareKind Records
Category: Music & DVDs
Average price: Modest
Address: 104 Trafalgar Street
Brighton BN1 4ER, UK
Phone: +44 1273 818170

#125
Levi Strauss & Co
Category: Fashion
Average price: Expensive
Address: Churchill Square Shopping Ctr
Brighton BN1 2RG, UK
Phone: +44 1273 725338

#126
Purple Heart
Category: Flowers & Gifts, Home Decor, Children's Clothing
Average price: Modest
Address: 19 North Street
Brighton BN1 1AH, UK
Phone: +44 1273 773310

#127
Kissing Fish
Category: Arts & Crafts, Flowers & Gifts, Home Decor
Average price: Modest
Address: 18 Gardner St
Brighton BN1 1UP, UK
Phone: +44 1273 606600

#128
Vegetarian Shoes
Category: Shoe Store
Average price: Expensive
Address: 12 Gardner St
Brighton BN1 1UP, UK
Phone: +44 1273 691913

#129
Kurt Geiger
Category: Shoe Store
Average price: Expensive
Address: 1-2 North Street
Brighton BN41 1DH, UK
Phone: +44 1273 749727

#130
Jack Wills
Category: Men's Clothing, Women's Clothing
Average price: Expensive
Address: 55 East Street
Brighton BN1 1JT, UK
Phone: +44 1273 748057

#131
Lombok
Category: Furniture Store, Home Decor, Mattresses
Average price: Expensive
Address: 6-7 North Street
Brighton BN1 1EB, UK
Phone: +44 845 241 8908

#132
Freedom Bikes
Category: Bikes
Average price: Modest
Address: 46-47 George Street
Brighton BN2 1RJ, UK
Phone: +44 1273 681698

#133
Sainsbury's
Category: Drugstore, Grocery, Bakery
Average price: Modest
Address: 93 Lewes Road
Brighton BN2 3QA, UK
Phone: +44 1273 674201

#134
Pardon My French
Category: Flowers & Gifts, Women's Clothing, Home Decor
Average price: Modest
Address: 15 St Georges Road
Brighton BN2 1EA, UK
Phone: +44 1273 694479

#135
Elm Grove Pharmacy
Category: Drugstore
Average price: Modest
Address: 74 Elm Grove
Brighton BN2 3DD, UK
Phone: +44 1273 606031

#136
Deans
Category: Electronics
Average price: Modest
Address: 29 St James Street
Brighton BN2 1RF, UK
Phone: +44 1273 601550

#137
Booth Museum of Natural History
Category: Museum, Art Gallery
Average price: Inexpensive
Address: 194 Dyke Road
Brighton BN1 5AA, UK
Phone: +44 30 0029 0200

#138
Neals Yard Remedies
Category: Health & Medical, Cosmetics & Beauty Supply
Average price: Expensive
Address: 2a Kensington Gardens
Brighton BN1 4AL, UK
Phone: +44 1273 601464

#139
Brighton Fishing Museum
Category: Museum, Art Gallery
Average price: Modest
Address: 201 Kings Road Arches
Brighton BN1 1NB, UK
Phone: +44 1273 723064

#140
Heal's
Category: Furniture Store
Average price: Expensive
Address: 1-2 Duke Street
Brighton BN1 1AH, UK
Phone: +44 1273 827300

#141
Dirty Harry
Category: Fashion
Average price: Inexpensive
Address: 6 Sydney St
Brighton BN1 4EN, UK
Phone: +44 1273 607527

#142
Cologne & Cotton
Category: Kitchen & Bath, Home Decor, Cosmetics & Beauty Supply
Average price: Expensive
Address: 13 Pavilion Buildings
Brighton BN1 1EE, UK
Phone: +44 1273 729666

#143
Oriental Arts
Category: Arts & Crafts, Home Decor
Average price: Inexpensive
Address: 14 Rock Street
Brighton BN2 1NF, UK
Phone: +44 1273 819168

#144
Zara
Category: Women's Clothing, Men's Clothing
Average price: Modest
Address: 56 Churchill Sq
Brighton BN1 2RG, UK
Phone: +44 1237 40180

#145
Great Expectations
Category: Baby Gear & Furniture
Average price: Modest
Address: 42-44 Lewes Rd
Brighton BN2 3HQ, UK
Phone: +44 1273 622993

#146
Marks & Spencer
Category: Department Store
Average price: Modest
Address: 195-200 Western Rd
Brighton BN1 2BJ, UK
Phone: +44 1273 328081

#147
Jojo Maman Bébé
Category: Maternity Wear, Baby Gear & Furniture
Average price: Expensive
Address: 40 Gardner St
Brighton BN1 1UN, UK
Phone: +44 1273 625682

#148
Noa Noa
Category: Women's Clothing
Average price: Expensive
Address: 37 Gardner Street
Brighton BN1 1UN, UK
Phone: +44 1273 818133

#149
To Be Worn Again
Category: Vintage & Consignment, Men's Clothing, Women's Clothing
Average price: Modest
Address: 24 Sydney Street
Brighton BN1 4EN, UK
Phone: +44 1273 680296

#150
Villa & Hut
Category: Furniture Store
Average price: Modest
Address: 40 Sydney Street
Brighton BN1 4EP, UK
Phone: +44 1273 696787

#151
Poundstretcher
Category: Outlet Store, Home & Garden
Average price: Inexpensive
Address: 46-47 London Road
Brighton BN1 4JD, UK
Phone: +44 1273 685450

#152
Schuh Shoes
Category: Shoe Store
Average price: Modest
Address: 34-35 Churchill Sq
Brighton BN1 2TD, UK
Phone: +44 1273 208483

#153
Reiss
Category: Fashion
Average price: Expensive
Address: 67 East St
Brighton BN1 1HQ, UK
Phone: +44 1273 770702

#154
Paperchase
Category: Cards & Stationery
Average price: Modest
Address: 66 East St
Brighton BN1 1HQ, UK
Phone: +44 1273 739150

#155
Bellis
Category: Art Gallery
Average price: Modest
Address: 8-9 King's Rd
Brighton BN1 1NE, UK
Phone: +44 1273 747429

#156
Silver
Category: Home Decor,
Arts & Crafts, Furniture Store
Average price: Modest
Address: 38 St James's St
Brighton BN2 1RG, UK
Phone: +44 1273 606909

#157
The Works
Category: Bookstore, Toy Store
Average price: Inexpensive
Address: 41-42 Western Road
Brighton BN1 2EB, UK
Phone: +44 1273 327421

#158
InHouse Space
Category: Home Decor,
Furniture Store, Flowers & Gifts
Average price: Modest
Address: 28 Gloucester Road
Brighton BN1 4AQ, UK
Phone: +44 1273 682845

#159
Graffiti
Category: Cards & Stationery
Average price: Modest
Address: 8 Cranbourne Street
Brighton BN1 2RD, UK
Phone: +44 1273 327777

#160
Jell-o
Category: Women's Clothing,
Men's Clothing
Average price: Expensive
Address: 16 Gardner Street
Brighton BN1 1UP, UK
Phone: +44 1273 609363

#161
Starfish
Category: Vintage & Consignment
Average price: Modest
Address: 25 Gardner St
Brighton BN1 1UP, UK
Phone: +44 1273 680868

#162
Nola Boutique
Category: Women's Clothing
Average price: Expensive
Address: 42 Gardner Street
Brighton BN1 1UN, UK
Phone: +44 1273 911006

#163
Vans Store
Category: Sports Wear, Shoe Store
Average price: Modest
Address: 38 West St
Brighton BN1 2RE, UK
Phone: +44 1273 777378

#164
Brighton Guitars
Category: Musical Instruments
Average price: Inexpensive
Address: 44 Sydney Street
Brighton BN1 4EP, UK
Phone: +44 1273 628444

#165
Daisy Daisy
Category: Baby Gear, Furniture & Toy Store
Average price: Modest
Address: 33 Sydney St
Brighton BN1 4EP, UK
Phone: +44 1273 571145

#166
Oxfam
Category: Books, Music & Video, Vintage & Consignment
Average price: Inexpensive
Address: 136 Western Road
Brighton BN1 2LA, UK
Phone: +44 1273 297435

#167
Sydney Street Bikes
Category: Bikes
Average price: Modest
Address: 24 Sydney Street
Brighton BN1 4EN, UK
Phone: +44 1273 624700

#168
All That Glitters
Category: Jewelry
Average price: Modest
Address: 9 Meeting House Lane
Brighton BN1 1HB, UK
Phone: +44 1273 733217

#169
Poundland
Category: Home & Garden, Cosmetics & Beauty Supply
Average price: Inexpensive
Address: Western Rd
Brighton BN1 2BB, UK
Phone: +44 1273 328801

#170
Snow & Rock
Category: Sports Wear
Average price: Expensive
Address: 54-55 Market Street
Brighton BN1 1HH, UK
Phone: +44 1273 827660

#171
PDSA
Category: Thrift Store
Average price: Inexpensive
Address: 12 Oxford St
Brighton BN1 4LA, UK
Phone: +44 1273 676552

#172
Masquerade
Category: Costumes
Average price: Expensive
Address: 40 Preston Road
Brighton BN1 4QF, UK
Phone: +44 1273 673381

#173
B & Q
Category: Hardware Store, Electronics
Average price: Modest
Address: Lewes Rd
Brighton BN2 3QA, UK
Phone: +44 1273 679926

#174
Daniel Laurence Home & Garden
Category: Framing, Home Decor
Average price: Expensive
Address: 226 Kings Rd Arches
Brighton BN1 1NB, UK
Phone: +44 1273 739694

#175
Igigi Women's Boutique
Category: Women's Clothing
Average price: Expensive
Address: 37 Western Road
Brighton BN3 1AF, UK
Phone: +44 1273 734160

#176
Altjeringa
Category: Accessories, Jewelry
Average price: Expensive
Address: 70 Western Rd
Brighton BN3 2JQ, UK
Phone: +44 1273 777956

#177
Vitas Footwear
Category: Shoe Store
Average price: Expensive
Address: 33 Gardner Street
Brighton BN1 1UN, UK
Phone: +44 1273 571175

#178
The Mole
Category: Men's Clothing, Sports Wear
Average price: Expensive
Address: 23 Kensington Gardens
Brighton BN1 4AL, UK
Phone: +44 1273 622282

#179
Crane Kalman Brighton
Category: Art Gallery
Average price: Expensive
Address: 38 Kensington Gardens
Brighton BN1 4AL, UK
Phone: +44 1273 697096

#180
Frame Factory
Category: Framing
Average price: Modest
Address: 7 Sydney Street
Brighton BN1 4EN, UK
Phone: +44 1273 609207

#181
People Tree
Category: Women's Clothing, Men's Clothing
Average price: Modest
Address: 35-36 West St
Brighton BN1 2RE, UK
Phone: +44 1273 328805

#182
Rina Tairo
Category: Jewelry
Average price: Expensive
Address: 13 Prince Albert Street
Brighton BN1 1HE, UK
Phone: +44 1273 774288

#183
Burnetts
Category: Newspapers & Magazines, Convenience Store
Average price: Modest
Address: 62 Preston Street
Brighton BN1 2HE, UK
Phone: +44 1273 329545

#184
Karen Millen
Category: Women's Clothing, Accessories
Average price: Expensive
Address: 5 Nile Street
Brighton BN1 1HW, UK
Phone: +44 1273 220581

#185
Ted Baker
Category: Fashion
Average price: Expensive
Address: 19-20 Dukes Lane
Brighton BN1 1BG, UK
Phone: +44 1273 202181

#186
Market Flower Shop
Category: Florist
Average price: Inexpensive
Address: 9 Open Market
Brighton BN1 4JS, UK
Phone: +44 1273 690726

#187
She Said
Category: Women's Clothing, Adult
Average price: Modest
Address: 11 Ship St Gardens
Brighton BN1 1AJ, UK
Phone: +44 1273 777811

#188
To Be Worn Again
Category: Vintage & Consignment
Average price: Modest
Address: 51 Providence Place
Brighton BN1 4GE, UK
Phone: +44 1273 624500

#189
O2 Store
Category: Electronics, Mobile Phones
Average price: Expensive
Address: 95 Churchill Square
Brighton BN1 2TB, UK
Phone: +44 1273 725721

#190
Nua
Category: Adult
Average price: Modest
Address: 59a Ship Street
Brighton BN1 1AE, UK
Phone: +44 1273 774001

#191
Kissmekwik
Category: Cards & Stationery
Average price: Modest
Address: 4 George Street
Brighton BN2 1RH, UK
Phone: +44 1273 571757

#192
Alexander Gallery
Category: Art Gallery, Arts & Crafts
Average price: Modest
Address: 7 East St
Brighton BN1 1HP, UK
Phone: +44 1273 321694

#193
Dean's
Category: Electronics
Average price: Modest
Address: 29 St James's Street
Brighton BN2 1RF, UK
Phone: +44 1273 601550

#194
Rayment Cycles
Category: Bikes
Average price: Expensive
Address: 13-14 Circus Parade
Brighton BN1 4GW, UK
Phone: +44 1273 697617

#195
Prowler
Category: Men's Clothing, Adult
Average price: Modest
Address: 112 St James's St
Brighton BN2 1TH, UK
Phone: +44 1273 683680

#196
Brighton Books
Category: Bookstore
Average price: Modest
Address: 18 Kensington Gardens
Brighton BN1 4AL, UK
Phone: +44 1273 693845

#197
Lust!
Category: Lingerie, Adult
Average price: Modest
Address: 43 Gardner Street
Brighton BN1 1UN, UK
Phone: +44 1273 699344

#198
Crystals
Category: Jewelry
Average price: Modest
Address: 35 Sydney Street
Brighton BN1 4EP, UK
Phone: +44 1273 626726

#199
Fat Face
Category: Fashion
Average price: Modest
Address: 51 Ship St
Brighton BN1 1AF, UK
Phone: +44 1273 736228

#200
Cargo Homeshop
Category: Home Decor, Furniture Store
Average price: Expensive
Address: 16 - 17 North Street
Brighton BN1 1EB, UK
Phone: +44 1273 733953

#201
Kemp Town Bookshop
Category: Bookstore, Coffee & Tea
Average price: Modest
Address: 91 St George's Road
Brighton BN2 1EE, UK
Phone: +44 1273 682110

#202
Eleventh Flower
Category: Florist
Average price: Modest
Address: 259 Ditchling Road
Brighton BN1 6JH, UK
Phone: +44 1273 706005

#203
Marie Curie Cancer Care
Category: Thrift Store
Average price: Inexpensive
Address: 99 St Georges Road
Brighton BN2 1EE, UK
Phone: +44 1273 673695

#204
Two Feathers
Category: Arts & Crafts, Jewelry
Average price: Modest
Address: 11 Kensington Gardens
Brighton BN1 4AL, UK
Phone: +44 1273 692929

#205
Retail Therapy
Category: Flowers & Gifts
Average price: Modest
Address: 101 Gloucester Rd
Brighton BN1 4AP, UK
Phone: +44 1273 691720

#206
Immediate Clothing
Category: Vintage & Consignment
Average price: Modest
Address: 34 Sydney Street
Brighton BN1 4EP, UK
Phone: +44 1273 603844

#207
Dance 2 Records
Category: Music & DVDs, Electronics
Average price: Modest
Address: 129 Western Rd
Brighton BN1 2AD, UK
Phone: +44 1273 220023

#208
Oasis Stores
Category: Women's Clothing
Average price: Modest
Address: 12-14 Dukes Lane
Brighton BN1 1BG, UK
Phone: +44 1273 323492

#209
Art At Five
Category: Art Gallery
Average price: Expensive
Address: 5 Bartholomews
Brighton BN1 1HG, UK
Phone: +44 1273 774222

#210
Games Workshop
Category: Computers
Average price: Modest
Address: 7 Nile Street
Brighton BN1 1HW, UK
Phone: +44 1273 203333

#211
Music Room
Category: Musical Instruments
Average price: Modest
Address: 90 Western Road
Brighton BN3 1, UK
Phone: +44 1273 775607

#212
Apple Store
Category: Computers
Average price: Expensive
Address: Upper Mall
Brighton BN1 2TE, UK
Phone: +44 1273 740500

#213
Jessops
Category: Photography Store, Electronics, Electronics Repair
Average price: Expensive
Address: 125 Queens Rd
Brighton BN1 3WB, UK
Phone: +44 1273 321492

#214
Octopus
Category: Home & Garden, Flowers & Gifts
Average price: Modest
Address: 16-17 Cranbourne St
Brighton BN1 2RD, UK
Phone: +44 1273 774078

#215
Eco Logic Cool
Category: Flowers & Gifts
Average price: Modest
Address: 46 Sydney Street
Brighton BN1 4EP, UK
Phone: +44 1273 606077

#216
One In The House
Category: Cards & Stationery, Home Decor
Average price: Modest
Address: 40 Trafalgar St
Brighton BN1 4ED, UK
Phone: +44 1273 677714

#217
Gamestation
Category: Books, Mags, Music & Video
Average price: Modest
Address: 69 Western Road
Brighton BN1 2HA, UK
Phone: +44 1273 220029

#218
Wildcat
Category: Adult
Average price: Modest
Address: 6 Gardner Street
Brighton BN1 1UP, UK
Phone: +44 1273 323758

#219
Toby Tiger
Category: Children's Clothing, Baby Gear & Furniture
Average price: Modest
Address: 11 Gardner St
Brighton BN1 1UP, UK
Phone: +44 1273 693000

#220
To Be Worn Again
Category: Vintage & Consignment
Average price: Expensive
Address: 12 Kensington Gardens
Brighton BN1 4, UK
Phone: +44 1273 687811

#221
Boy Parker
Category: Men's Clothing, Women's Clothing
Average price: Expensive
Address: 6 Kensington Gardens
Brighton BN1 4AL, UK
Phone: +44 1273 687766

#222
Lily Lv
Category: Women's Clothing
Average price: Modest
Address: 12a Bond Street
Brighton BN1 1RD, UK
Phone: +44 1273 724420

#223
Bonsai Ko
Category: Nursery & Gardening
Average price: Modest
Address: 45 Sydney Street
Brighton BN1 4EP, UK
Phone: +44 1273 621743

#224
Mail Boxes Etc.
Category: Office Equipment
Average price: Modest
Address: 91 Western Road
Brighton BN1 2NW, UK
Phone: +44 1273 706020

#225
Market Place
Category: Fashion, Jewelry
Average price: Inexpensive
Address: 6-8 Meeting House Lane
Brighton BN1 1HB, UK
Phone: +44 1273 329417

#226
Partytime
Category: Party Supplies
Average price: Inexpensive
Address: 107-108 London Rd
Brighton BN1 4JG, UK
Phone: +44 1273 695606

#227
WH Smith
Category: Bookstore, Office Equipment, Music & DVDs
Average price: Modest
Address: Unit 2 Churchill Sq
Brighton BN1 2TA, UK
Phone: +44 1273 324146

#228
Hove YMCA
Category: Thrift Store, Furniture Store
Average price: Modest
Address: 67 London Rd
Brighton BN1 4JE, UK
Phone: +44 1273 261944

#229
Accessorize
Category: Accessories
Average price: Expensive
Address: Unit 16 Churchill Sq
Brighton BN1 2TB, UK
Phone: +44 1273 823944

#230
Badlands Guitars
Category: Musical Instruments
Average price: Modest
Address: 48 Preston Rd
Brighton BN1 4QF, UK
Phone: +44 1273 673363

#231
Boots
Category: Drugstore
Average price: Modest
Address: 17-19 St James's St
Brighton BN2 1RF, UK
Phone: +44 1273 682308

#232
Paros Antiques
Category: Antiques
Average price: Modest
Address: 35 Upper ST James's Street
Brighton BN2 1JN, UK
Phone: +44 1273 696737

#233
H&M
Category: Women's Clothing, Men's Clothing, Children's Clothing
Average price: Inexpensive
Address: 181-185 Western Rd
Brighton BN1 2BG, UK
Phone: +44 1273 827020

#234
Velvet
Category: Interior Design, Furniture Store, Women's Clothing
Average price: Expensive
Address: 66-68 Church Rd
Brighton BN3 2FP, UK
Phone: +44 1273 725992

#235
White Stuff
Category: Women's Clothing, Men's Clothing, Outdoor Gear
Average price: Modest
Address: Unit C
Brighton BN1 3GJ, UK
Phone: +44 1273 747368

#236
Willow
Category: Women's Clothing, Accessories
Average price: Modest
Address: 80 George Street
Brighton BN3 3YE, UK
Phone: +44 1273 202452

#237
Peacocks
Category: Men's Clothing, Women's Clothing
Average price: Modest
Address: 134 North Street
Brighton BN1 1RG, UK
Phone: +44 1273 772479

#238
Office
Category: Shoe Store
Average price: Modest
Address: 5-6 Cranbourne Street
Brighton BN1 2RD, UK
Phone: +44 1273 205609

#239
Rococo
Category: Costumes
Average price: Expensive
Address: 26 Gardner Street
Brighton BN1 1UP, UK
Phone: +44 1273 698415

#240
Appendage Fashion Shop
Category: Fashion, Home Decor
Average price: Modest
Address: 36 Kensington Gardens
Brighton BN1 4AL, UK
Phone: +44 1273 605901

#241
Sensation
Category: Jewelry
Average price: Expensive
Address: 15 Kensington Gardens
Brighton BN1 4AL, UK
Phone: +44 1273 605913

#242
Fullertons
Category: Cards & Stationery
Average price: Modest
Address: 151 Dyke Rd
Brighton BN1 3JE, UK
Phone: +44 1273 325508

#243
The Singles Bar
Category: Music & Video
Average price: Inexpensive
Address: 28A Tidy St
Brighton BN1 4EL, UK
Phone: +44 1273 673744

#244
Hope and Harlequin
Category: Bridal, Women's Clothing
Average price: Expensive
Address: 31 Sydney St
Brighton BN1 4EP, UK
Phone: +44 1273 675222

#245
HMV
Category: Books, Mags, Music & Video
Average price: Modest
Address: 48-50 Churchill Square Shopping Ctr, Brighton BN1 2RG, UK
Phone: +44 843 221 0136

#246
R W Berry & Son
Category: Furniture Store, Home Decor, Antiques
Average price: Modest
Address: 120 Dyke Road Brighton BN1 3TE, UK
Phone: +44 1273 326326

#247
Peggs and Son
Category: Men's Clothing, Shoe Store
Average price: Expensive
Address: 39 Duke Street Brighton BN1 1AG, UK
Phone: +44 1273 711847

#248
The Shelter Charity Shop
Category: Home & Garden, Vintage & Consignment
Average price: Modest
Address: 93 Western Rd Brighton BN1 2LB, UK
Phone: +44 1273 710581

#249
Artist Residence
Category: Art Gallery, Guest House
Average price: Modest
Address: 33 Regency Sq Brighton BN1 2GG, UK
Phone: +44 1273 324302

#250
Churchill Square Shopping Centre
Category: Shopping Center
Average price: Modest
Address: Russell Place Brighton BN1 2RG, UK
Phone: +44 1273 327428

#251
Papillon
Category: Home Decor
Average price: Expensive
Address: 8 Union Street Brighton BN1 1HA, UK
Phone: +44 1273 720333

#252
Norfolk News
Category: Newspapers & Magazines
Average price: Inexpensive
Address: 110c Western Rd Brighton BN1 2AA, UK
Phone: +44 1273 732920

#253
Tickled
Category: Adult
Average price: Modest
Address: 59 Ship St Brighton BN1 1AE, UK
Phone: +44 1273 777822

#254
Mariposa
Category: Arts & Crafts, Home Decor
Average price: Expensive
Address: 6 Brighton Pl Brighton BN1 1HJ, UK
Phone: +44 1273 328171

#255
Help the Aged
Category: Thrift Store
Average price: Inexpensive
Address: 21 London Rd Brighton BN1 4JB, UK
Phone: +44 1273 607605

#256
Diamond Hardware
Category: Computers
Average price: Modest
Address: 36 New England Rd Brighton BN1 4GG, UK
Phone: +44 1273 625032

#257
Sallis Benney Theatre
Category: Performing Arts, Art Gallery
Average price: Modest
Address: 58-67 Grand Parade Brighton BN2 0JY, UK
Phone: +44 1273 600900

#258
Mostyns
Category: Fabric Store
Average price: Inexpensive
Address: 72-73 London Road
Brighton BN1 4JE, UK
Phone: +44 1273 606360

#259
David Clulow
Category: Eyewear & Opticians
Average price: Expensive
Address: 25 East Street
Brighton BN1 1HL, UK
Phone: +44 1273 737578

#260
Molton Brown Cosmetics
Category: Cosmetics & Beauty Supply
Average price: Expensive
Address: 60 East St
Brighton BN1 1HN, UK
Phone: +44 1273 730115

#261
All Saints
Category: Fashion
Average price: Expensive
Address: 62-63 East Street
Brighton BN1 1HQ, UK
Phone: +44 1273 710107

#262
Republic Retail
Category: Women's Clothing, Men's Clothing
Average price: Modest
Address: Unit 80 Churchill Square
Brighton BN1 2TF, UK
Phone: +44 1273 749764

#263
Long Tall Sally
Category: Accessories
Average price: Modest
Address: 10 East Street
Brighton BN1 1HP, UK
Phone: +44 1273 731791

#264
Coast
Category: Women's Clothing
Average price: Modest
Address: 59 East Street
Brighton BN1 1HN, UK
Phone: +44 1273 821305

#265
Cry Of The Gulls
Category: Art Gallery
Average price: Modest
Address: 32 Meeting House Lane
Brighton BN1 1HB, UK
Phone: +44 1273 734347

#266
Kemp Town Tools
Category: Hardware Store
Average price: Modest
Address: 46-47 George Street
Brighton BN2 1RJ, UK
Phone: +44 1273 672769

#267
Amsterdammers
Category: Bikes
Average price: Modest
Address: 39 Open Market
Brighton BN1 4JS, UK
Phone: +44 1273 571555

#268
Superdrug
Category: Drugstore, Cosmetics & Beauty Supply
Average price: Modest
Address: 27-28 St James's St
Brighton BN2 1RF, UK
Phone: +44 1273 607211

#269
Next
Category: Women's Clothing, Men's Clothing, Children's Clothing
Average price: Modest
Address: 46-47 Upper Mall Churchill Square, Brighton BN1 2TE, UK
Phone: +44 1273 327307

#270
Lovely Jubbly
Category: Antiques, Furniture Store
Average price: Inexpensive
Address: 14 Lewes Rd
Brighton BN2 3, UK
Phone: +44 1273 699655

#271
Two Kats & A Cow
Category: Art Gallery
Average price: Expensive
Address: 167 Kings Rd Arches
Brighton BN1 1NB, UK
Phone: +44 1273 776746

#272
Seafront Image
Category: Cards & Stationery
Average price: Expensive
Address: 195 Kings Rd Arches
Brighton BN1 1NB, UK
Phone: +44 1273 725777

#273
HD2 Brighton
Category: Music & DVDs
Average price: Inexpensive
Address: 91 St James's Street
Brighton BN2 1TP, UK
Phone: +44 1273 608488

#274
Planted Florists
Category: Florist
Average price: Modest
Address: 90 St James Street
Brighton BN2 1TT, UK
Phone: +44 1273 699911

#275
Boxbird Gallery
Category: Art Gallery
Average price: Modest
Address: 14 St. John's Rd
Brighton BN3 2FB, UK
Phone: +44 1273 734295

#276
Linens Direct
Category: Furniture Store, Home Decor
Average price: Inexpensive
Address: 48 Western Rd
Brighton BN1 2EB, UK
Phone: +44 1273 722491

#277
Loot
Category: Women's Clothing, Men's Clothing, Vintage & Consignment
Average price: Modest
Address: 25 Gloucester Rd
Brighton BN1 4, UK
Phone: +44 1273 697300

#278
Evolution Brighton Bond
Category: Home Decor, Gift Shop
Average price: Modest
Address: 42 Bond Street
Brighton BN1 1RD, UK
Phone: +44 1273 205379

#279
Kate Langdale Interiors and Floral Design
Category: Interior and Floral Design
Average price: Expensive
Address: 84 Dyke Rd
Brighton BN1 3, UK
Phone: +44 7944 756277

#280
Brighton Sewing Centre
Category: Arts & Crafts
Average price: Modest
Address: 68 North Rd
Brighton BN1 1YD, UK
Phone: +44 1273 621653

#281
Guttersnipes Clothing
Category: Women's Clothing, Men's Clothing
Average price: Modest
Address: 94a Gloucester Rd
Brighton BN1 4AP, UK
Phone: +44 1273 670555

#282
Fruity
Category: Women's Clothing
Average price: Modest
Address: 18 Tichborne Street
Brighton BN1 1UR, UK
Phone: +44 1273 321231

#283
Utility
Category: Hardware Store
Average price: Modest
Address: 28A North Rd
Brighton BN1 1YB, UK
Phone: +44 1273 626222

#284
Silverado
Category: Jewelry
Average price: Modest
Address: 31 Bond Street
Brighton BN1 1RD, UK
Phone: +44 1273 735040

#285
Envy
Category: Fashion
Average price: Expensive
Address: 57 Churchill Square
Brighton BN1 2TE, UK
Phone: +44 1273 204544

#286
Penelope's Portmanteau
Category: Vintage Bags & Handbags
Average price: Inexpensive
Address: 42A Ship Street
Brighton BN1 1AF, UK
Phone: +44 1273 737171

#287
Aldo
Category: Shoe Store
Average price: Expensive
Address: Churchill Square
Brighton BN1 2RG, UK
Phone: +44 1273 760011

#288
The Studio Shop
Category: Arts & Crafts
Average price: Modest
Address: 15 Montpelier Pl
Brighton BN1 3BF, UK
Phone: +44 1273 732005

#289
D & A
Category: Eyewear & Opticians
Average price: Modest
Address: 39 London Road
Brighton BN1 4JB, UK
Phone: +44 1273 698142

#290
Go Botanica
Category: Florist
Average price: Modest
Address: Queens Rd
Brighton BN1 3XP, UK
Phone: +44 7740 724734

#291
Russell & Bromley
Category: Shoe Store
Average price: Expensive
Address: 57-58 East Street
Brighton BN1 1HN, UK
Phone: +44 1273 326772

#292
Rose Florist
Category: Florist, Nursery & Gardening
Average price: Modest
Address: 63 Ditchling Rd
Brighton BN1 4SD, UK
Phone: +44 1273 696624

#293
Leonie Claire
Category: Fashion, Bridal
Average price: Expensive
Address: 46 Upper North Street
Brighton BN1 3FH, UK
Phone: +44 1273 711458

#294
Velo Vitality
Category: Bikes
Average price: Modest
Address: 44 Trafalgar Street
Brighton BN1 4ED, UK
Phone: +44 1273 699184

#295
High & Mighty
Category: Men's Clothing
Average price: Modest
Address: 132 Queens Rd
Brighton BN1 3WB, UK
Phone: +44 1273 325677

#296
Paint Pots
Category: Home Decor
Average price: Modest
Address: 39 Trafalgar Street
Brighton BN1 4ED, UK
Phone: +44 1273 696682

#297
Seven Dials Music
Category: Musical Instruments
Average price: Modest
Address: 41 Prestonville Road
Brighton BN1 3TJ, UK
Phone: +44 1273 775780

#298
Retro
Category: Antiques, Hobby Shop
Average price: Expensive
Address: 7-8 Kensington Gardens
Brighton BN1 4AL, UK
Phone: +44 7884 231861

#299
Fidra Jewellers
Category: Jewelry
Average price: Expensive
Address: 47 Meeting House Lane
Brighton BN1 1HB, UK
Phone: +44 1273 328348

#300
Ashtons
Category: Drugstore
Average price: Modest
Address: 98 Dyke Rd
Brighton BN1 3JD, UK
Phone: +44 1273 325020

#301
Frame of Mind
Category: Framing, Art Gallery
Average price: Modest
Address: 2A Blatchington Rd
Brighton BN3 3YN, UK
Phone: +44 1273 776329

#302
Trafalgar House Engraving
Category: Jewelry, Accessories
Average price: Inexpensive
Address: 4 Trafalgar Street
Brighton BN1 4EQ, UK
Phone: +44 1273 603498

#303
Leoframes
Category: Arts & Crafts
Average price: Expensive
Address: 70 North Rd
Brighton BN1 1YD, UK
Phone: +44 1273 695862

#304
Brighton Architectural Salvage
Category: Home & Garden
Average price: Expensive
Address: 33-34 Gloucester Rd
Brighton BN1 4AQ, UK
Phone: +44 1273 681656

#305
Brighton Arts Club
Category: Art Gallery, Social Club, Party & Event Planning
Average price: Modest
Address: 43 Providence Place
Brighton BN1 4GE, UK
Phone: +44 7757 781957

#306
Flawless
Category: Sports Wear, Men's Clothing, Women's Clothing
Average price: Modest
Address: 20 Kensington Gardens
Brighton BN1 4AL, UK
Phone: +44 1273 688484

#307
Curiouser & Curiouser
Category: Jewelry
Average price: Modest
Address: 2 Sydney Street
Brighton BN1 4EN, UK
Phone: +44 1273 673120

#308
St George's Store
Category: Newspapers & Magazines
Average price: Modest
Address: 139 Western Rd
Brighton BN1 2LA, UK
Phone: +44 1273 325375

#309
Tribeca
Category: Women's Clothing
Average price: Expensive
Address: 21 Bond Street
Brighton BN1 1RD, UK
Phone: +44 1273 673755

#310
The Body Shop
Category: Cosmetics & Beauty Supply
Average price: Modest
Address: 41-43 North Street
Brighton BN1 1RH, UK
Phone: +44 1273 327048

#311
Hampstead Bazaar
Category: Women's Clothing
Average price: Expensive
Address: 10 Bond St
Brighton BN1 1RD, UK
Phone: +44 1273 207712

#312
Top Shop
Category: Fashion
Average price: Modest
Address: 179-180 Western Road
Brighton BN1 2BA, UK
Phone: +44 1273 774611

#313
Chameleon Gallery
Category: Art Gallery
Average price: Expensive
Address: 13a Prince Albert St
Brighton BN1 1HE, UK
Phone: +44 1273 324432

#314
Cult Retail
Category: Men's Clothing, Women's Clothing
Average price: Expensive
Address: Unit 1 North Street
Brighton BN1 1RG, UK
Phone: +44 1273 774298

#315
Gamestar
Category: Video Game Rental
Average price: Modest
Address: 45 London Road
Brighton BN1 4JD, UK
Phone: +44 1273 688886

#316
Smokemart
Category: Newspapers & Magazines
Average price: Inexpensive
Address: 45 London Road
Brighton BN1 4JD, UK
Phone: +44 1273 680594

#317
Posh Totty Designs Boutique
Category: Women's Clothing, Accessories, Jewelry
Average price: Modest
Address: 1 Bond St Cottages
Brighton BN1 1RP, UK
Phone: +44 1273 202044

#318
Witch Ball
Category: Antiques, Home Decor
Average price: Modest
Address: 48 Meeting House Lane
Brighton BN1 1HB, UK
Phone: +44 1273 326618

#319
Colourstream
Category: Photography Store
Average price: Modest
Address: 123 St James's Street
Brighton BN2 1TH, UK
Phone: +44 1273 683030

#320
Bravissimo
Category: Sports Wear, Swimwear
Average price: Expensive
Address: 3 North St
Brighton BN1 1EB, UK
Phone: +44 1273 731540

#321
Corner Shop Collectables
Category: Antiques, Fashion
Average price: Inexpensive
Address: 30 Bristol Rd
Brighton BN2 1AP, UK
Phone: +44 1273 690974

#322
Brighton Framing Gallery
Category: Framing, Art Gallery
Average price: Modest
Address: 103 St Georges Rd
Brighton BN2 1EA, UK
Phone: +44 1273 696221

#323
Now We Are Six
Category: Toy Store
Average price: Modest
Address: 44 Church Rd
Brighton BN3 2EB, UK
Phone: +44 1273 722533

#324
New & Second-Hand Discount Furniture
Category: Furniture Store
Average price: Modest
Address: 137-138 Lewes Road
Brighton BN2 3LG, UK
Phone: +44 1273 243776

#325
Fairtrade Gallery
Category: Art Gallery, Framing
Average price: Modest
Address: 26 Montague Pl
Brighton BN2 1JE, UK
Phone: +44 7990 511576

#326
Prescription Art
Category: Art Gallery
Average price: Modest
Address: 16 - 30 Hollingdean Road
Brighton BN2 4AA, UK
Phone: +44 7941 385715

#327
Sports Direct
Category: Sports Wear
Average price: Modest
Address: 134-138 North St
Brighton BN1 1RG, UK
Phone: +44 870 333 9540

#328
King Of Rock
Category: T Shirts, Memorabilia
Average price: Modest
Address: 24 North St
Brighton BN1 1EB, UK
Phone: +44 1273 730492

#329
Samaritans
Category: Thrift Store
Average price: Inexpensive
Address: 70 George St
Brighton BN3 3YD, UK
Phone: +44 1273 711254

#330
Well Done
Category: Newspapers & Magazines
Average price: Modest
Address: 14 Pavilion Buildings
Brighton BN1 1EE, UK
Phone: +44 1273 777606

#331
Clinton Cards
Category: Cards & Stationery
Average price: Expensive
Address: Unit 39 Churchill Square
Brighton BN1 2TD, UK
Phone: +44 1273 711559

#332
River Island
Category: Fashion
Average price: Modest
Address: Unit 59 Churchill Square
Brighton BN1 2TE, UK
Phone: +44 1273 726604

#333
Cissy Mo
Category: Home & Garden, Arts & Crafts
Average price: Expensive
Address: 38 Sydney St
Brighton BN1 4EP, UK
Phone: +44 1273 607777

#334
Cyberdog
Category: Men's Clothing,
Women's Clothing, Accessories
Average price: Modest
Address: 13 Sydney St
Brighton BN1 4EN, UK
Phone: +44 1273 677961

#335
Hank and Hugo
Category: Gift Shop
Average price: Expensive
Address: 115 St Georges Road
Brighton BN2 1EA, UK
Phone: +44 1273 684023

#336
Step Back In Time
Category: Antiques, Hobby Shop
Average price: Modest
Address: 125 Queens Road
Brighton BN1 3WB, UK
Phone: +44 1273 731883

#337
Ann Summers
Category: Adult, Lingerie
Average price: Modest
Address: 30-31 Western Rd
Brighton BN1 2EB, UK
Phone: +44 870 053 4007

#338
Cool Hand Luke
Category: Men's Clothing
Average price: Inexpensive
Address: 29 Gloucester Rd
Brighton BN1 4AQ, UK
Phone: +44 1273 686496

#339
Modelzone
Category: Hobby Shop, Toy Store
Average price: Modest
Address: 37 West Street
Brighton BN1 2RE, UK
Phone: +44 1273 326790

#340
Loaded
Category: Men's Clothing,
Women's Clothing
Average price: Modest
Address: 6 Kensington Gardens
Brighton BN1 4AL, UK
Phone: +44 1273 687802

#341
Two Way Book Exchange
Category: Bookstore
Average price: Inexpensive
Address: 54 Gardner Street
Brighton BN1 1UN, UK
Phone: +44 1273 687729

#342
Tantalus
Category: Accessories, Jewelry
Average price: Expensive
Address: 28 Bond Street
Brighton BN1 1RD, UK
Phone: +44 1273 738828

#343
Spiral Sussex
Category: Furniture Store, Vintage & Consignment
Average price: Inexpensive
Address: 103A Bedford Pl
Brighton BN1 2AA, UK
Phone: +44 1273 763960

#344
The Body Shop
Category: Cosmetics & Beauty Supply
Average price: Modest
Address: 41-43 N Street
Brighton BN1 1RH, UK
Phone: +44 1273 327048

#345
Shu-Time
Category: Shoe Store
Average price: Inexpensive
Address: 33 London Road
Brighton BN1 4JB, UK
Phone: +44 1273 686373

#346
The Royal Pavilion Shop
Category: Cards & Stationery
Average price: Modest
Address: 5 Pavilion Buildings
Brighton BN1 1EE, UK
Phone: +44 1273 292798

#347
Yellow Shop
Category: Gift Shop
Average price: Modest
Address: 9 Oxford Street
Brighton BN1 4LA, UK
Phone: +44 1273 685773

#348
Florentin
Category: Home Decor
Average price: Modest
Address: 2 Pool Valley
Brighton BN1 1NJ, UK
Phone: +44 1273 777887

#349
Passport Menswear
Category: Men's Clothing
Average price: Modest
Address: 108 St James St
Brighton BN2 1TH, UK
Phone: +44 1273 621422

#350
Superdrug
Category: Drugstore, Cosmetics
Average price: Modest
Address: Churchill Square Shopping Ctr
Brighton BN1 2TF, UK
Phone: +44 1273 739562

#351
Asda
Category: Grocery, Department Store
Average price: Modest
Address: Brighton Marina
Brighton BN2 5UT, UK
Phone: +44 1273 606611

#352
Gap
Category: Women's Clothing, Men's Clothing
Average price: Modest
Address: 192 Western Road
Brighton BN1 2BA, UK
Phone: +44 1273 220032

#353
Bo Peeps
Category: Home Decor, Furniture Store
Average price: Modest
Address: 27 Duke St
Brighton BN1 1AG, UK
Phone: +44 7850 546726

#354
Brighton Lanes Antique Centre
Category: Antiques, Jewelry
Average price: Expensive
Address: 12 Meeting House Lane
Brighton BN1 1HB, UK
Phone: +44 1273 823121

#355
United Colors of Benetton
Category: Women's Clothing, Men's Clothing, Accessories
Average price: Modest
Address: 8-9 North Street
Brighton BN1 1EB, UK
Phone: +44 1273 730491

#356
Fired Earth
Category: Kitchen & Bath
Average price: Expensive
Address: 15c Prince Albert Street
Brighton BN1 1HF, UK
Phone: +44 1273 719977

#357
Astro
Category: Books, Mags, Music & Video, Electronics
Average price: Modest
Address: 44 Gardner Street
Brighton BN1 1UN, UK
Phone: +44 1273 603538

#358
New Look
Category: Fashion
Average price: Modest
Address: 187 Western Rd
Brighton BN1 2BA, UK
Phone: +44 1273 729225

#359
Expo
Category: Home Decor, Cards & Stationery, Art Gallery
Average price: Modest
Address: Churchill Sq
Brighton BN1 2TF, UK
Phone: +44 1273 726347

#360
The Red Gecko
Category: Home & Garden, Arts & Crafts
Average price: Modest
Address: 13 East St
Brighton BN1 1HP, UK
Phone: +44 1273 325593

#361
Evolution Clearance
Category: Accessories, Home Decor
Average price: Inexpensive
Address: 89 Western Rd
Brighton BN3 1, UK
Phone: +44 1273 727123

#362
The Boozy Cow
Category: Convenience Store
Average price: Modest
Address: St. Georges St
Brighton BN2 1EB, UK
Phone: +44 1273 604786

#363
St Vincent de Paul Society
Category: Thrift Store
Average price: Inexpensive
Address: 162-164 Louis Road
Brighton BN2 3GU, UK
Phone: +44 1273 501114

#364
The O Zone
Category: Bridal
Average price: Expensive
Address: 21-23 Church St
Brighton BN1 1RB, UK
Phone: +44 1273 739500

#365
Sirene
Category: Women's Clothing
Average price: Expensive
Address: 37 Trafalgar St
Brighton BN1 4ED, UK
Phone: +44 1273 818061

#366
Bluedog Gallery
Category: Art Gallery
Average price: Expensive
Address: 20 Gardner Street
Brighton BN1 1UP, UK
Phone: +44 1273 622440

#367
Peter Davey & Son
Category: Home & Garden
Average price: Modest
Address: 18 Sydney Street
Brighton BN1 4EN, UK
Phone: +44 1273 690512

#368
Flawless Kicks
Category: Shoe Store
Average price: Modest
Address: 22 Bond St
Brighton BN1 1RD, UK
Phone: +44 1273 819492

#369
Brothers Retail Convenience Store
Category: Convenience Store, Grocery
Average price: Modest
Address: 92 Western Rd
Brighton BN1 2LB, UK
Phone: +44 1273 777264

#370
Trafalgar News
Category: Tobacco Shop
Average price: Modest
Address: 95 Trafalgar Street
Brighton BN1 4ER, UK
Phone: +44 1273 696459

#371
Cult Hero
Category: Bookstore
Average price: Modest
Address: 25 North Street
Brighton BN1 1EB, UK
Phone: +44 1273 771959

#372
Prism
Category: Kitchen & Bath
Average price: Modest
Address: 10 Meeting House Lane
Brighton BN1 1HB, UK
Phone: +44 1273 204088

#373
The Wishing Well
Category: Jewelry
Average price: Inexpensive
Address: 46 Baker Street
Brighton BN1 4JN, UK
Phone: +44 1273 695950

#374
Wallis
Category: Women's Clothing
Average price: Modest
Address: Churchill Square Shopping Ctr
Brighton BN1 2TE, UK
Phone: +44 1273 332 6944

#375
Paperchase
Category: Cards & Stationery
Average price: Modest
Address: Borders
Brighton BN1 2TB, UK
Phone: +44 1273 731122

#376
Bone Idol
Category: Sporting Goods
Average price: Modest
Address: 125 Kings Rd Arches
Brighton BN1 2FN, UK
Phone: +44 1273 770666

#377
Ouh La La
Category: Lingerie
Average price: Expensive
Address: 71 N Road
Brighton BN1 1YD, UK
Phone: +44 1273 699888

#378
Grandad's Bike Shop
Category: Bikes
Average price: Modest
Address: 14 Elm Grove
Brighton BN2 3DD, UK
Phone: +44 1273 685650

#379
Robert John Featherbe
Category: Antiques
Average price: Modest
Address: 2 Clyde Road
Brighton BN1 4NP, UK
Phone: +44 1273 673041

#380
In Retrospect
Category: Antique
Average price: Expensive
Address: 37 Upper ST. James's Street
Brighton BN2 1JN, UK
Phone: +44 1273 609374

#381
Classical Lighting
Category: Home Decor, Home Cleaning
Average price: Modest
Address: 123 - 124 Western Road
Brighton BN1 2AD, UK
Phone: +44 1273 771899

#382
Ryman The Stationer
Category: Office Equipment
Average price: Expensive
Address: 55 North Street
Brighton BN1 1RH, UK
Phone: +44 1273 775306

#383
Julian Stephens Goldsmiths
Category: Jewelry
Average price: Modest
Address: 37 Gloucester Road
Brighton BN1 4AQ, UK
Phone: +44 1273 692110

#384
Moda & Soda
Category: Fashion
Average price: Modest
Address: 7 Gardner St
Brighton BN1 1UP, UK
Phone: +44 1273 682994

#385
Fashion Temple
Category: Women's Clothing
Average price: Modest
Address: 19 Trafalgar Street
Brighton BN1 4EQ, UK
Phone: +44 1273 605498

#386
Storm
Category: Jewelry
Average price: Modest
Address: 5 Bond St
Brighton BN1 1RD, UK
Phone: +44 1273 736822

#387
Badger
Category: Jewelry, Women's Clothing
Average price: Expensive
Address: 25 Bond Street
Brighton BN1 1RD, UK
Phone: +44 1273 325421

#388
North Street Food & Wine
Category: Newspapers & Magazines
Average price: Inexpensive
Address: 23 North Street
Brighton BN1 1EB, UK
Phone: +44 1273 327599

#389
Jaffa Hair
Category: Accessories
Average price: Expensive
Address: 19-20 Meeting House Lane
Brighton BN1 1HB, UK
Phone: +44 1273 730154

#390
Argos
Category: Shopping
Average price: Modest
Address: 157-163 Western Road
Brighton BN1 2BB, UK
Phone: +44 845 165 7132

#391
Yoma
Category: Women's Clothing, Accessories, Shoe Store
Average price: Modest
Address: 39 Gardner Street
Brighton BN1 1UN, UK
Phone: +44 1273 571455

#392
Claire's Accessories UK
Category: Accessories
Average price: Modest
Address: Unit 24 Churchill Sq
Brighton BN1 2TD, UK
Phone: +44 1273 202400

#393
Claire's Accessories UK
Category: Accessories
Average price: Inexpensive
Address: 6
Brighton Square
Brighton BN1 1HD, UK
Phone: +44 1273 326505

#394
WH Smith
Category: Bookstore
Average price: Expensive
Address: Queens Rd
Brighton BN1 3ZE, UK
Phone: +44 1273 328561

#395
Clarks
Category: Shoe Store
Average price: Modest
Address: 51-52 Churchill Sq
Brighton BN1 2TE, UK
Phone: +44 844 499 5473

#396
Videostar
Category: Videos & Video Game Rental
Average price: Modest
Address: 60 Saint James's Street
Brighton BN2 1QG, UK
Phone: +44 1273 690935

#397
Oxfam Bookshop
Category: Books, Mags, Music & Video
Average price: Inexpensive
Address: 47 Blatchington Rd
Brighton BN3 3YJ, UK
Phone: +44 1273 733163

#398
Carpetright
Category: Home & Garden
Average price: Inexpensive
Address: Pelham Terrace Lewes Rd
Brighton BN2 4AF, UK
Phone: +44 844 248 5732

#399
M & A Convenience Store
Category: Convenience Store
Average price: Expensive
Address: 140-141 Lewes Rd
Brighton BN2 3LG, UK
Phone: +44 1273 605141

#400
Ivy's Menswear Specialist
Category: Men's Clothing
Average price: Inexpensive
Address: 33 Church Street
Brighton BN1 1RL, UK
Phone: +44 1273 328587

#401
Three Angels Interiors Antiques
Category: Antiques
Average price: Expensive
Address: 86 Dyke Road
Brighton BN1 3JD, UK
Phone: +44 1273 711009

#402
Appendage
Category: Arts & Crafts, Jewelry
Average price: Expensive
Address: 36 Kensington Gardens
Brighton BN1 4AL, UK
Phone: +44 1273 605901

#403
PS Brighton
Category: Bookstore
Average price: Inexpensive
Address: 34 Kensington Gardens
Brighton BN1 4AL, UK
Phone: +44 1273 468433

#404
Dollond & Aitchison
Category: Eyewear & Opticians
Average price: Modest
Address: 82 Churchill Square
Brighton BN1 2TF, UK
Phone: +44 1273 325548

#405
Kate & Aud
Category: Women's Clothing, Vintage & Consignment
Average price: Expensive
Address: 27 Trafalgar St
Brighton BN1 4ED, UK
Phone: +44 7533 581344

#406
Scandecor
Category: Furniture Store
Average price: Modest
Address: 20 Castle Street
Brighton BN1 2HD, UK
Phone: +44 1273 820208

#407
Lookfantastic
Category: Hair Salons, Cosmetics & Beauty Supply
Average price: Expensive
Address: 16 Duke Street
Brighton BN1 1AH, UK
Phone: +44 1273 328787

#408
Woodies Exclusive Fashions
Category: Men's Clothing
Average price: Expensive
Address: 20-21 Duke Street
Brighton BN1 1AH, UK
Phone: +44 1273 776777

#409
Natural Alternative Decoration Centre
Category: Arts & Crafts
Average price: Modest
Address: Gloucester House, 45 Gloucester Street Brighton BN1 4EW, UK
Phone: +44 1273 685800

#410
Baroque Jewellery
Category: Jewelry
Average price: Expensive
Address: 9 Union Street
Brighton BN1 1HA, UK
Phone: +44 1273 777003

#411
Hedonizm Records
Category: Music & DVDs
Average price: Modest
Address: 106 Trafalgar Street
Brighton BN1 4ER, UK
Phone: +44 1273 700061

#412
RING
Category: Jewelry
Average price: Modest
Address: 21 Meeting House Lane
Brighton BN1 1HB, UK
Phone: +44 1273 773544

#413
Brighton Bookstack
Category: Bookstore
Average price: Modest
Address: 4 North Street
Brighton BN1 1EB, UK
Phone: +44 1273 721212

#414
M L Banfield & Sons
Category: Hardware Store
Average price: Modest
Address: 1-2 Little Western St
Brighton BN1 2QH, UK
Phone: +44 1273 737622

#415
L'Occitane
Category: Health Markets, Cosmetics & Beauty Supply
Average price: Expensive
Address: 23a East St
Brighton BN1 1HL, UK
Phone: +44 1273 719171

#416
Boath Audio Visual
Category: Electronics, Party Supplies
Average price: Modest
Address: 42 New England Road
Brighton BN1 4GG, UK
Phone: +44 1273 600678

#417
Jaeger
Category: Men's Clothing
Average price: Expensive
Address: 12 Pavilion Buildings
Brighton BN1 1EE, UK
Phone: +44 1273 736430

#418
Baker Street Framing
Category: Framing
Average price: Modest
Address: 32 Baker Street
Brighton BN1 4JN, UK
Phone: +44 1273 680650

#419
North Star Studio Printmaking Co-Operative
Category: Art Gallery, Professional Services
Average price: Inexpensive
Address: 65 Ditchling Rd
Brighton BN1 4SD, UK
Phone: +44 1273 601041

#420
MBI Sound & Light
Category: Electronics
Average price: Modest
Address: 168 Edward St
Brighton BN2 0JB, UK
Phone: +44 1273 607384

#421
R J Featherbe
Category: Antiques
Average price: Inexpensive
Address: 2 Clyde Road
Brighton BN1 4NP, UK
Phone: +44 1273 673041

#422
Studio Bookshop
Category: Bookstore
Average price: Modest
Address: 68 ST James's Street
Brighton BN2 1PJ, UK
Phone: +44 1273 691253

#423
Stephen Bower Pharmacy
Category: Drugstore
Average price: Inexpensive
Address: 109 St James's Street
Brighton BN2 1TH, UK
Phone: +44 1273 681715

#424
Shoe Zone
Category: Shoe Store
Average price: Inexpensive
Address: 84-85 Western Rd
Brighton BN1 2HA, UK
Phone: +44 1273 778635

#425
Pullingers
Category: Shoe Store
Average price: Modest
Address: 9 Bond St
Brighton BN1 1RD, UK
Phone: +44 1273 725476

#426
The White Company
Category: Home Decor, Children's Clothing
Average price: Modest
Address: 4 North St
Brighton BN1 1EB, UK
Phone: +44 845 678 8150

#427
99p Store
Category: Discount Store
Average price: Inexpensive
Address: 27-31 London Road
Brighton BN1 4LE, UK
Phone: +44 1273 603279

#428
H & M Hennes
Category: Men's Clothing, Women's Clothing
Average price: Modest
Address: Unit 79 Churchill Sq
Brighton BN1 2TF, UK
Phone: +44 1273 729743

#429
JAG Studio & Gallery
Category: Art Gallery
Average price: Modest
Address: 283A Madeira Dr
Brighton BN2 1PT, UK
Phone: +44 7810 523984

#430
Wigwam
Category: Toy Store
Average price: Inexpensive
Address: 140 Preston Drove
Brighton BN1 6FJ, UK
Phone: +44 1273 505504

#431
Furniture Hut
Category: Furniture Store
Average price: Inexpensive
Address: 190-193 Lewes Rd
Brighton BN2 3LA, UK
Phone: +44 1273 603741

#432
Bik Chief
Category: Shoe Store
Average price: Inexpensive
Address: 14 Gardner St
Brighton BN1 1UP, UK
Phone: +44 1273 670705

#433
Light Settings
Category: Home Decor
Average price: Modest
Address: 53 North St
Brighton BN1 1RH, UK
Phone: +44 1273 739720

#434
Sweets N Things
Category: Newspapers & Magazines
Average price: Inexpensive
Address: 100B Western Rd
Brighton BN1 2AA, UK
Phone: +44 1273 711744

#435
Framing Studio
Category: Framing
Average price: Modest
Address: 30 Upper North Street
Brighton BN1 3FG, UK
Phone: +44 1273 731405

#436
The Argus
Category: Newspapers & Magazines
Average price: Inexpensive
Address: 2 Castle Sq
Brighton BN1 1EG, UK
Phone: +44 1273 321045

#437
Fashion Temple
Category: Women's Clothing
Average price: Modest
Address: 163 Western Rd
Brighton BN1 2BB, UK
Phone: +44 1273 731310

#438
North Laine Hair
Category: Cosmetics & Beauty Supply, Blow Dry/Out Services
Average price: Modest
Address: 38 Gardner Street
Brighton BN1 1UN, UK
Phone: +44 1273 607057

#439
Phones 4U
Category: Mobile Phones
Average price: Modest
Address: 62 North Street
Brighton BN1 1SQ, UK
Phone: +44 1273 773415

#440
Miss Selfridge
Category: Women's Clothing, Accessories
Average price: Modest
Address: 4 Churchill Square
Brighton BN1 2TA, UK
Phone: +44 1273 324294

#441
Silver Scene
Category: Jewelry
Average price: Modest
Address: 14 Prince Albert Street
Brighton BN1 1HE, UK
Phone: +44 1273 779288

#442
Sunderland Electronics
Category: Electronics
Average price: Modest
Address: 51-52 Norfolk Sq
Brighton BN1 2PA, UK
Phone: +44 1273 774113

#443
Strudwick Cycles
Category: Bikes
Average price: Inexpensive
Address: 28 Oxford Street
Brighton BN1 4LA, UK
Phone: +44 1273 609015

#444
Dorothy Perkins
Category: Women's Clothing, Accessories
Average price: Modest
Address: Unit 50 Churchill Sq
Brighton BN1 2TE, UK
Phone: +44 1273 731250

#445
Tom Wolfe
Category: Men's Clothing
Average price: Modest
Address: Churchill Sq
Brighton BN1 2TE, UK
Phone: +44 1273 719731

#446
USC Group
Category: Men's Clothing
Average price: Modest
Address: Unit 72 Churchill Square
Brighton BN1 2TB, UK
Phone: +44 1273 733457

#447
Warehouse
Category: Women's Clothing
Average price: Modest
Address: Churchill Square Shopping Ctr
Brighton, UK
Phone: +44 1273 204815

#448
French Connection
Category: Men's Clothing
Average price: Modest
Address: 55 East Street
Brighton BN1 1JT, UK
Phone: +44 1273 727117

#449
Al-Amin Exotic Foods
Category: Ethnic Food, Wholesale Store
Average price: Modest
Address: 9 Lewes Road
Brighton BN2 3HP, UK
Phone: +44 1273 687695

#450
Ponden Home Superstore
Category: Home Decor
Average price: Modest
Address: Lewes Rd
Brighton BN2 3QA, UK
Phone: +44 1273 694433

#451
Run
Category: Women's Clothing, Men's Clothing, Shoe Store
Average price: Modest
Address: 46 Blatchington Rd
Brighton BN3 3YH, UK
Phone: +44 1273 770972

#452
Waterstones
Category: Bookstore
Average price: Modest
Address: 71-74 North Street
Brighton BN1 1ZA, UK
Phone: +44 1273 206017

#453
Whittard of Chelsea
Category: Home Decor
Average price: Modest
Address: 14 Churchill Sq
Brighton BN1, UK
Phone: +44 1273 726283

#454
Giftzstore
Category: Flowers & Gifts
Average price: Inexpensive
Address: 13 Brighton Square
Brighton BN1 1HD, UK
Phone: +44 1273 737003

#455
Action Bikes
Category: Bikes
Average price: Modest
Address: 93 London Road
Brighton BN1 4JF, UK
Phone: +44 1273 605160

#456
Bhs
Category: Department Store
Average price: Modest
Address: Churchill Square
Brighton BN1 2TA, UK
Phone: +44 1273 324383

#457
Booze Box
Category: Music & DVDs,
Beer, Wine & Spirits
Average price: Inexpensive
Address: 2 Queens Parade
Brighton BN3 8JG, UK
Phone: +44 1273 772622

#458
Paver Shoes
Category: Shoe Store
Average price: Inexpensive
Address: Unit 10 The Waterfront
Brighton BN2 5WA, UK
Phone: +44 1273 693713

#459
Bon Marche
Category: Women's Clothing
Average price: Modest
Address: 8 London Rd
Brighton BN1 4JA, UK
Phone: +44 1273 628456

#460
L.K.
Category: Women's Clothing
Average price: Modest
Address: 38 East Street
Brighton BN1 1HL, UK
Phone: +44 1273 722988

#461
Gloucester Newsagents
Category: Newspapers & Magazines
Average price: Modest
Address: 107 Gloucester Road
Brighton BN1 4AP, UK
Phone: +44 1273 695801

#462
The Magazine Shop
Category: Newspapers & Magazines
Average price: Modest
Address: 122 Dyke Road
Brighton BN1 3TE, UK
Phone: +44 1273 321345

#463
Ampwitch
Category: Music & DVDs
Average price: Modest
Address: 22 Trafalgar St
Brighton BN1 4EQ, UK
Phone: +44 1273 687968

#464
Simultane
Category: Fashion
Average price: Modest
Address: 52 Ship Street
Brighton BN1 1AF, UK
Phone: +44 1273 777535

#465
Edwards & Hope
Category: Appliances
Average price: Modest
Address: 5 New Road
Brighton BN1 1UF, UK
Phone: +44 1273 775166

#466
King Of GSM
Category: Mobile Phones
Average price: Inexpensive
Address: 72 Preston Street
Brighton BN1 2HG, UK
Phone: +44 7787 806043

#467
Peacocks
Category: Women's Clothing
Average price: Inexpensive
Address: 1 5-8 London Road
Brighton BN1 4JA, UK
Phone: +44 1273 571547

#468
Shell World
Category: Flowers & Gifts, Arts & Crafts
Average price: Inexpensive
Address: 41 Kings Road
Brighton BN1 1NA, UK
Phone: +44 1273 327664

#469
The Musicbox
Category: Musical Instruments
Average price: Modest
Address: 16 Baker Street
Brighton BN1 4JN, UK
Phone: +44 1273 677767

#470
C & H Weston
Category: Outdoor Gear, Hobby Shop
Average price: Modest
Address: 12 East Street
Brighton BN1 1HP, UK
Phone: +44 1273 326338

#471
Tony Young Autographs
Category: Shopping
Average price: Modest
Address: 138 Edward Street
Brighton BN2 0JL, UK
Phone: +44 1273 732418

#472
Ignition
Category: Adult
Average price: Modest
Address: 8 Blatchington Rd
Brighton BN3 3YH, UK
Phone: +44 1273 321888

#473
D M S News
Category: Newspapers & Magazines
Average price: Modest
Address: 185 Elm Grove
Brighton BN2 3EL, UK
Phone: +44 1273 681170

#474
Savery Antiques & Books
Category: Bookstore
Average price: Inexpensive
Address: 257 Ditchling Road
Brighton BN1 6JH, UK
Phone: +44 1273 564899

#475
News & Needs
Category: Newspapers & Magazines
Average price: Modest
Address: 22 Bear Road
Brighton BN2 4DA, UK
Phone: +44 1273 607022

#476
Sharps Pharmacy
Category: Drugstore
Average price: Inexpensive
Address: 26 Coombe Road
Brighton BN2 4EA, UK
Phone: +44 1273 604384

#477
Boots Opticians
Category: Eyewear & Opticians
Average price: Modest
Address: 129 North St
Brighton BN1 2BE, UK
Phone: +44 1273 207461

#478
Don Marche
Category: Women's Clothing
Average price: Modest
Address: 151-152 Western Rd
Brighton BN1 2DA, UK
Phone: +44 1273 770740

#479
T Chest
Category: Women's Clothing, Men's Clothing
Average price: Modest
Address: 13 Gardner Street
Brighton BN1 1UP, UK
Phone: +44 1273 620950

#480
Framework
Category: Art Gallery
Average price: Modest
Address: 26 Kensington Gardens
Brighton BN1 4AL, UK
Phone: +44 1273 818585

#481
Bellerophon
Category: Antiques
Average price: Modest
Address: 96 Trafalgar Street
Brighton BN1 4ER, UK
Phone: +44 7904 391327

#482
Potters Children Store
Category: Toy Store
Average price: Modest
Address: 41 Meeting House Lane
Brighton BN1 1HB, UK
Phone: +44 1273 820900

#483
Clinton Cards
Category: Cards & Stationery
Average price: Modest
Address: 20 London Rd
Brighton BN1 4JB, UK
Phone: +44 1273 625100

#484
Crabtree & Evelyn
Category: Cosmetics & Beauty Supply
Average price: Modest
Address: 22 East St
Brighton BN1 1HL, UK
Phone: +44 1273 712810

#485
Krisp Clothing
Category: Women's Clothing
Average price: Inexpensive
Address: Unit 8 Churchill Square
Brighton BN1 2TA, UK
Phone: +44 1273 779997

#486
Monsoon
Category: Fashion
Average price: Modest
Address: 42 East Street
Brighton BN1 1HL, UK
Phone: +44 1273 734352

#487
ODM Office Discount Megastore
Category: Office Equipment, Computers
Average price: Inexpensive
Address: 235-237 Hangleton Rd
Brighton BN3 7LR, UK
Phone: +44 1273 203100

#488
Pen to Paper
Category: Cards & Stationery
Average price: Modest
Address: 4 Sydney Street
Brighton BN1 4EN, UK
Phone: +44 1273 676670

#489
Booker Cash & Carry
Category: Discount Store
Average price: Inexpensive
Address: Moulsecoomb Way
Brighton BN2 4NP, UK
Phone: +44 1273 624242

#490
Oxfam Bookshop
Category: Books, Mags,
Music & Video, Thrift Store
Average price: Inexpensive
Address: 30 Kensington Gardens
Brighton BN1 4AL, UK
Phone: +44 1273 698093

#491
Pink
Category: Fashion
Average price: Modest
Address: 41 Bond Street
Brighton BN1 1RD, UK
Phone: +44 1273 327758

#492
Bell, Book & Candle
Category: Hobby Shop,
Flowers & Gifts, Bookstore
Average price: Modest
Address: 38 Gardner Street
Brighton BN1 1UN, UK
Phone: +44 1273 818101

#493
Caia Matheson Artist
Category: Art Gallery
Average price: Modest
Address: Beaconsfield Studio
Brighton BN1 4QL, UK
Phone: +44 7961 405351

#494
Add The Colour
Category: Coffee & Tea, Art Gallery
Average price: Inexpensive
Address: 64-65 North Road
Brighton BN1 1YD, UK
Phone: +44 7817 850202

#495
Quince
Category: Florist
Average price: Modest
Address: 2 Nile Street
Brighton BN1 1HW, UK
Phone: +44 1273 227004

#496
Phones 4U
Category: Mobile Phones
Average price: Modest
Address: 40 Western Road
Brighton BN1 2EB, UK
Phone: +44 1273 328191

#497
Kemptown Trading Post & Cafe
Category: Coffee & Tea, Antiques
Average price: Modest
Address: 28 St Georges Road
Brighton BN2 1, UK
Phone: +44 1273 698873

#498
Creased Cards
Category: Cards & Stationery
Average price: Modest
Address: 6 Meeting House Lane
Brighton BN1 1HB, UK
Phone: +44 1273 321718

#499
Scent The Florist
Category: Flowers & Gifts
Average price: Modest
Address: 101 Gloucester Rd
Brighton BN1 4AP, UK
Phone: +44 1273 607600

#500
Saki Miu
Category: Women's Clothing, Furniture Store
Average price: Modest
Address: 27 Kensington Gardens
Brighton BN1 4AL, UK
Phone: +44 1273 67949

TOP 500 RESTAURANTS

Recommended by Locals & Trevelers

(From #1 to #500)

#1
Lydea
Cuisines: Vegetarian
Average price: Under $10
Address: 17 Kensington Gardens
Brighton BN1 4AL, UK
Phone: +44 1273 667992

#2
Casa Don Carlos
Cuisines: Spanish, Tapas Bar
Average price: $11-30
Address: 5 Union Street
Brighton BN1 1HA, UK
Phone: +44 1273 327177

#3
Riddle & Finns
Cuisines: Seafood, Champagne Bar
Average price: $31-60
Address: 12 Meeting House Lane
Brighton BN1 1HB, UK
Phone: +44 1273 721667

#4
Foodilic
Cuisines: Buffet, Food
Average price: Under $10
Address: 60 North Street
Brighton BN1 1RH, UK
Phone: +44 1273 774138

#5
The Gingerman
Cuisines: British, Food
Average price: $31-60
Address: 21a Norfolk Square
Brighton BN1 2PD, UK
Phone: +44 1273 326688

#6
Basketmakers Arms
Cuisines: Pub, British, Food
Average price: Under $10
Address: 12 Gloucester Road
Brighton BN1 4AD, UK
Phone: +44 1273 689006

#7
Bill's
Cuisines: Fruits & Veggies, British, Breakfast & Brunch
Average price: $11-30
Address: 100 North Road
Brighton BN1 1YE, UK
Phone: +44 1273 692894

#8
Bom-Bane's
Cuisines: Coffee & Tea, Belgian
Average price: $31-60
Address: 24 George Street
Brighton BN2 1RH, UK
Phone: +44 1273 606400

#9
The Chilli Pickle
Cuisines: Indian
Average price: $11-30
Address: 17 Jubilee Street
Brighton BN1 1GE, UK
Phone: +44 1273 900383

#10
Terre A Terre
Cuisines: Vegetarian, Food
Average price: $31-60
Address: 71 East Street
Brighton BN1 1HQ, UK
Phone: +44 1273 729051

#11
La Cave à Fromage
Cuisines: Cheese Shop, French
Average price: $11-30
Address: 34-35 Western Road
Brighton BN3 1AF, UK
Phone: +44 1273 725500

#12
Warung Tujuh
Cuisines: Indonesian, Fast Food
Average price: $11-30
Address: 7 Pool Valley
Brighton BN1 1NJ, UK
Phone: +44 1273 720784

#13
La Cucina
Cuisines: Pizza
Average price: $11-30
Address: 4a Montpelier Place
Brighton BN1 3BF, UK
Phone: +44 1273 202206

#14
Northern Lights
Cuisines: Scandinavian, Pub
Average price: $11-30
Address: 6 Little E Street
Brighton BN1 1HT, UK
Phone: +44 1273 747096

#15
Sushi Garden
Cuisines: Japanese, Sushi Bar
Average price: $31-60
Address: 32a-33a Preston Street
Brighton BN1 2HP, UK
Phone: +44 1273 727246

#16
Hop Poles
Cuisines: Pub, British
Average price: $11-30
Address: 13 Middle Street
Brighton BN1 1AL, UK
Phone: +44 1273 207566

#17
Food For Friends
Cuisines: Vegetarian, Coffee & Tea
Average price: $11-30
Address: 17-18 Prince Albert Street
Brighton BN1 1HF, UK
Phone: +44 1273 202310

#18
Pompoko
Cuisines: Japanese
Average price: Under $10
Address: 110 Church Street
Brighton BN1 1UD, UK
Phone: +44 7796 001927

#19
Moshimo
Cuisines: Japanese, Sushi Bar
Average price: $11-30
Address: The Opticon Bartholomew Square
Brighton BN1 1JS, UK
Phone: +44 1273 719195

#20
Grubbs Burgers
Cuisines: Fast Food, Burgers
Average price: Under $10
Address: 13 York Place
Brighton BN1 4GU, UK
Phone: +44 1273 691869

#21
Kensington Cafe
Cuisines: Breakfast & Brunch, British
Average price: Under $10
Address: 1a Kensington Gardens
Brighton BN1 4AL, UK
Phone: +44 1273 570963

#22
The Ginger Pig
Cuisines: GastroPub, French
Average price: $31-60
Address: 3 Hove Street
Brighton BN3 2TR, UK
Phone: +44 1273 736123

#23
The Burger Bar
Cuisines: Fast Food, British, Burgers
Average price: Under $10
Address: 11a Market Street
Brighton BN1 1HH, UK
Phone: +44 1273 205979

#24
Pizzaface
Cuisines: Pizza
Average price: $11-30
Address: 35 St Georges Road
Brighton BN2 1ED, UK
Phone: +44 1273 699082

#25
Sawadee
Cuisines: Thai
Average price: $11-30
Address: 87 ST. James's Street
Brighton BN2 1TP, UK
Phone: +44 1273 624233

#26
Sussex Yeoman
Cuisines: Pub, British
Average price: $31-60
Address: 7 Guildford Road
Brighton BN1 3LU, UK
Phone: +44 1273 327985

#27
Cocoa
Cuisines: Desserts, French
Average price: $11-30
Address: 48 Queens Road
Brighton BN1 3XB, UK
Phone: +44 1273 777412

#28
Toast
Cuisines: Sandwiches, Coffee & Tea,
Breakfast & Brunch
Average price: Under $10
Address: 38 Trafalgar Street
Brighton BN1 4ED, UK
Phone: +44 872 148 6121

#29
Jamie's Italian
Cuisines: Italian
Average price: $11-30
Address: 11 Black Lion St
Brighton BN1 1ND, UK
Phone: +44 1273 915480

#30
Browns Bar & Brasserie
Cuisines: British
Average price: $31-60
Address: 3-4 Duke St
Brighton BN1 1AH, UK
Phone: +44 1273 323501

#31
E-Kagen Sushi & Noodle Bar
Cuisines: Japanese
Average price: Under $10
Address: 22-23 Sydney Street
Brighton BN1 4EN, UK
Phone: +44 1273 687068

#32
The Setting Sun
Cuisines: Pub, GastroPub
Average price: $11-30
Address: 1 Windmill Street
Brighton BN2 0GN, UK
Phone: +44 1273 626192

#33
Moksha Caffe
Cuisines: Coffee & Tea, Sandwiches, Bakery
Average price: Under $10
Address: 4-5 York Placce
Brighton BN1 4GU, UK
Phone: +44 1273 248890

#34
Planet India
Cuisines: Indian, Food
Average price: Under $10
Address: 4-5 Richmond Parade
Brighton BN2 9PH, UK
Phone: +44 1273 818149

#35
The Windmill
Cuisines: Pub, British
Average price: $11-30
Address: 69 Upper North Street
Brighton BN1 3FL, UK
Phone: +44 1273 202475

#36
English's of Brighton
Cuisines: Seafood
Average price: $31-60
Address: 29 East Street
Brighton BN1 1HL, UK
Phone: +44 1273 327980

#37
MuraSaki
Cuisines: Japanese, Fast Food
Average price: $11-30
Address: 115 Dyke Road
Brighton BN1 3JE, UK
Phone: +44 1273 326231

#38
Mange Tout
Cuisines: French, Breakfast & Brunch
Average price: $11-30
Address: 81 Trafalgar Street
Brighton BN1 4EB, UK
Phone: +44 1273 607270

#39
Bona Foodie
Cuisines: Delis, Sandwiches
Average price: Above $61
Address: 21 ST James's Street
Brighton BN2 1RF, UK
Phone: +44 1273 698007

#40
Agra Tandoori Take Away
Cuisines: Fast Food, Indian
Average price: $11-30
Address: 263 Ditchling Road
Brighton BN1 6JH, UK
Phone: +44 1273 541652

#41
The Foragers
Cuisines: GastroPub, Pub, British
Average price: $11-30
Address: 3 Stirling Place
Brighton BN3 3YU, UK
Phone: +44 1273 733134

#42
Muang Thai Restaurant
Cuisines: Thai
Average price: $11-30
Address: 77 St James's Street
Brighton BN2 1PA, UK
Phone: +44 1273 605223

#43
Grubbs Burgers
Cuisines: Fast Food, Burgers
Average price: $11-30
Address: 89 St James's Street
Brighton BN2 1TP, UK
Phone: +44 1273 688111

#44
Estia
Cuisines: Greek, Mediterranean
Average price: $11-30
Address: 3 Hampton Place
Brighton BN1 3DA, UK
Phone: +44 1273 777399

#45
The Prince George
Cuisines: British, Pub, Vegetarian
Average price: $11-30
Address: 5 Trafalgar Street
Brighton BN1 4EQ, UK
Phone: +44 1273 681055

#46
The Dorset
Cuisines: Seafood, Pub
Average price: $11-30
Address: 28 North Road
Brighton BN1 1YB, UK
Phone: +44 1273 605423

#47
Mascara Restaurant
Cuisines: African
Average price: $11-30
Address: 101 Western Road
Brighton BN1 2AA, UK
Phone: +44 1273 278185

#48
The Greys
Cuisines: Pub, British
Average price: $11-30
Address: 105 Southover Street
Brighton BN2 9UA, UK
Phone: +44 1273 680734

#49
Sam's Of Brighton
Cuisines: British, Breakfast & Brunch
Average price: $11-30
Address: 1 Paston Place
Brighton BN2 1HA, UK
Phone: +44 1273 676222

#50
Krua Anne
Cuisines: Thai
Average price: Under $10
Address: 19 Kensington Gardens
Brighton BN1 4AL, UK
Phone: +44 1273 628555

#51
Sopar Thai Restaurant
Cuisines: Thai
Average price: $11-30
Address: 40 Upper St James Street
Brighton BN2 1JN, UK
Phone: +44 1273 628427

#52
River Spice
Cuisines: Indian
Average price: $11-30
Address: 17 Preston Street
Brighton BN1 2HN, UK
Phone: +44 1273 739183

#53
Toasters
Cuisines: Fast Food
Average price: $11-30
Address: 12 Market Street
Brighton BN1 1HH, UK
Phone: +44 7976 656293

#54
Temptation
Cuisines: Breakfast & Brunch
Average price: $11-30
Address: 56 Gardner Street
Brighton BN1 1UN, UK
Phone: +44 1273 673045

#55
Blenio Bistro
Cuisines: French, Coffee & Tea
Average price: $11-30
Address: 87 - 93 Dyke Road
Brighton BN1 3JE, UK
Phone: +44 1273 220220

#56
Earth And Stars
Cuisines: GastroPub
Average price: $11-30
Address: 46 Windsor Street
Brighton BN1 1RJ, UK
Phone: +44 1273 722879

#57
Regency Restaurant
Cuisines: Seafood
Average price: $11-30
Address: 131 Kings Road
Brighton BN1 2HH, UK
Phone: +44 1273 325014

#58
Fortune of War
Cuisines: Pub, Lounge, British
Average price: $11-30
Address: 157 Kings Road Arches
Brighton BN1 1NB, UK
Phone: +44 1273 205065

#59
Bardsley's Fish & Chips
Cuisines: Fish & Chips
Average price: Under $10
Address: 22-23a Baker Street
Brighton BN1 4JN, UK
Phone: +44 1273 681256

#60
Open House
Cuisines: Pub, GastroPub
Average price: $11-30
Address: 146 Springfield Road
Brighton BN1 6BZ, UK
Phone: +44 1273 880102

#61
Havana
Cuisines: Champagne Bar, Nightclub, European
Average price: Above $61
Address: 32 Duke Street
Brighton BN1 1AG, UK
Phone: +44 1273 773388

#62
Mai Ped Ped Ped
Cuisines: Thai, Tapas
Average price: $31-60
Address: 11a Market Street
Brighton BN1 1HH, UK
Phone: +44 1273 737373

#63
Rock Ola
Cuisines: American, Cafe
Average price: $11-30
Address: 29 Tidy Street
Brighton BN1 4EL, UK
Phone: +44 1273 673744

#64
The Old Bank Steak & Ribs
Cuisines: Steakhouse
Average price: $31-60
Address: 120 St George's Road
Brighton BN2 1EA, UK
Phone: +44 1273 682200

#65
Alfresco
Cuisines: Italian, Coffee & Tea
Average price: $31-60
Address: Kings Road Arches
Brighton BN1 2LN, UK
Phone: +44 1273 206523

#66
The Chimney House
Cuisines: GastroPub, Pub, British
Average price: $31-60
Address: 28 Upper Hamilton Road
Brighton BN1 5DF, UK
Phone: +44 1273 556708

#67
Planet India
Cuisines: Indian, Vegetarian, Fast Food
Average price: $11-30
Address: 4 Richmond Parade
Brighton BN2 9PH, UK
Phone: +44 1273 818149

#68
Las Iguanas
Cuisines: Lounge, Mexican, Brazilian
Average price: $11-30
Address: 7-8 Jubilee Street
Brighton BN1 1GE, UK
Phone: +44 1273 573550

#69
Melrose
Cuisines: Seafood
Average price: $11-30
Address: 132 Kings Road
Brighton BN1 2HH, UK
Phone: +44 1273 326520

#70
The Restaurant at Drakes
Cuisines: European
Average price: Above $61
Address: 43-44 Marine Parade
Brighton BN2 1PE, UK
Phone: +44 1273 696934

#71
L'Église
Cuisines: French
Average price: $31-60
Address: 196 Church Road
Brighton BN3 2DJ, UK
Phone: +44 1273 220868

#72
Red Snapper
Cuisines: Thai
Average price: $11-30
Address: 90 Dyke Road
Brighton BN1 3JD, UK
Phone: +44 1273 778866

#73
Olé Olé
Cuisines: Steakhouse, Spanish, Tapas
Average price: $11-30
Address: 42 Meeting House Lane
Brighton BN1 1HB, UK
Phone: +44 1273 739939

#74
Wagamama
Cuisines: Japanese
Average price: $31-60
Address: 93 North Road
Brighton BN1 1YE, UK
Phone: +44 1273 688892

#75
Farm
Cuisines: Coffee & Tea, Desserts, Breakfast & Brunch
Average price: Under $10
Address: 99 North Road
Brighton BN1 1YE, UK
Phone: +44 1273 623143

#76
Harry Ramsden's
Cuisines: Fish & Chips
Average price: Under $10
Address: 1-4 Marine Parade
Brighton BN2 1PA, UK
Phone: +44 1273 690691

#77
The Galley
Cuisines: Creperies, Sandwiches
Average price: Under $10
Address: 9 Church Street
Brighton BN1 1US, UK
Phone: +44 1273 724499

#78
Burger Brothers
Cuisines: Burgers
Average price: Under $10
Address: 97 North Road
Brighton BN1 1YE, UK
Phone: +44 1273 706980

#79
Solera
Cuisines: Spanish, Wine Bar, Tapas
Average price: $11-30
Address: 42 Sydney Street
Brighton BN1 4EP, UK
Phone: +44 1273 673966

#80
Plateau
Cuisines: Wine Bar, French, Tapas
Average price: $31-60
Address: 1 Bartholomews
Brighton BN1 1HG, UK
Phone: +44 1273 733085

#81
Pho
Cuisines: Vietnamese
Average price: $11-30
Address: 12 Black Lion Street
Brighton BN1 1ND, UK
Phone: +44 1273 202403

#82
Harvester
Cuisines: Steakhouse
Average price: $11-30
Address: 1 Madeira Drive
Brighton BN2 1PS, UK
Phone: +44 1273 573730

#83
New Steine Bistro
Cuisines: French, Breakfast & Brunch
Average price: $11-30
Address: 10 - 11 New Steine
Brighton BN2 1PB, UK
Phone: +44 1273 695415

#84
Fountain Head
Cuisines: Pub, GastroPub
Average price: $31-60
Address: 101-103 North Road
Brighton BN1 1YE, UK
Phone: +44 1273 628091

#85
Billie's
Cuisines: Breakfast & Brunch
Average price: Under $10
Address: 34 Hampton Place
Brighton BN1 3DD, UK
Phone: +44 1273 774386

#86
Bombay Aloo
Cuisines: Vegetarian, Indian
Average price: Under $10
Address: 39 Ship Street
Brighton BN1 1AB, UK
Phone: +44 1273 771089

#87
Coach House
Cuisines: British
Average price: $11-30
Address: 59 Middle Street
Brighton BN1 1AL, UK
Phone: +44 1273 719000

#88
Market Diner
Cuisines: Diners, Fast Food
Average price: Under $10
Address: 19-21 Circus Street
Brighton BN2 9QF, UK
Phone: +44 1273 608273

#89
The Mash Tun
Cuisines: Pub, British
Average price: $11-30
Address: 1 Church Street
Brighton BN1 1UE, UK
Phone: +44 1273 684951

#90
Istanbul Restaurant
Cuisines: Fast Food, Turkish
Average price: Under $10
Address: 125 Western Rd
Brighton BN1 2AD, UK
Phone: +44 1273 326699

#91
Bossa Nostra
Cuisines: Italian, Brazilian
Average price: $11-30
Address: 8 East Street
Brighton BN1 1HP, UK
Phone: +44 1273 711901

#92
Shahi Tandoori
Cuisines: Indian, Pakistani
Average price: $11-30
Address: 40-42 Beaconsfield Road
Brighton BN1 4QH, UK
Phone: +44 1273 626187

#93
Pavel
Cuisines: Indian
Average price: $11-30
Address: 40 St James Street
Brighton BN2 1RG, UK
Phone: +44 1273 692711

#94
Fishy Fishy
Cuisines: Seafood
Average price: $31-60
Address: 36 East St
Brighton BN1 1HL, UK
Phone: +44 1273 723750

#95
Archipelagos
Cuisines: Greek
Average price: $11-30
Address: 121 Western Road
Brighton BN3 1DB, UK
Phone: +44 1273 779474

#96
Druids Head
Cuisines: Pub, GastroPub
Average price: $11-30
Address: 9 Brighton Place
Brighton BN1 1HJ, UK
Phone: +44 1273 325490

#97
Bagelman
Cuisines: Sandwiches, Coffee & Tea
Average price: $31-60
Address: 31 Ship St
Brighton BN1 1AD, UK
Phone: +44 1273 772779

#98
Cafe Coho
Cuisines: Breakfast & Brunch, Cafe
Average price: $11-30
Address: 53 Ship Street
Brighton BN1 1AF, UK
Phone: +44 1273 747777

#99
El Mexicano
Cuisines: Mexican, Tex-Mex
Average price: $11-30
Address: 7 New Road
Brighton BN1 1UF, UK
Phone: +44 1273 727766

#100
Pub With No Name
Cuisines: Pub, GastroPub
Average price: $11-30
Address: 58 Southover Street
Brighton BN2 9UF, UK
Phone: +44 1273 601419

#101
Cafe Rouge
Cuisines: Coffee & Tea, French
Average price: $11-30
Address: 24 Prince Albert St
Brighton BN1 1HF, UK
Phone: +44 1273 774422

#102
The New Club
Cuisines: American
Average price: $11-30
Address: 133-134 Kings Road
Brighton BN1 2HH, UK
Phone: +44 1273 730320

#103
Circus Circus
Cuisines: Pub, Thai
Average price: $11-30
Address: 2 Preston Road
Brighton BN1 4QF, UK
Phone: +44 1273 620026

#104
The Cod Father
Cuisines: Fish & Chips
Average price: Under $10
Address: 109 Islingword Road
Brighton BN2 9SG, UK
Phone: +44 1273 699038

#105
Buddies Restaurant
Cuisines: Fish & Chips, Fast Food
Average price: $11-30
Address: 46 Kings Rd
Brighton BN1 1NA, UK
Phone: +44 1273 323600

#106
Pizza Express Restaurant
Cuisines: Pizza, Italian
Average price: $11-30
Address: 4 Waterfront
Brighton BN2 5WA, UK
Phone: +44 1273 689300

#107
The Laine Deli
Cuisines: Coffee & Tea, Sandwiches
Average price: Under $10
Address: 31 Trafalgar Street
Brighton BN1 4ED, UK
Phone: +44 1273 686665

#108
Steki's Taverna
Cuisines: Greek, Fast Food
Average price: $31-60
Address: 127 Kings Road
Brighton BN1 2FA, UK
Phone: +44 1273 730202

#109
The Medicine Chest
Cuisines: American, European
Average price: $31-60
Address: 51 - 55 Brunswick Street
Brighton BN3 1AU, UK
Phone: +44 1273 770002

#110
Seven Stars
Cuisines: Pub, GastroPub
Average price: $11-30
Address: 27 Ship St
Brighton BN1 1AD, UK
Phone: +44 1273 258800

#111
The Manor
Cuisines: Breakfast & Brunch
Average price: $11-30
Address: 52 Gardner St
Brighton BN1 1UN, UK
Phone: +44 1273 691700

#112
Little Bay Restaurant
Cuisines: French, Mediterranean
Average price: $11-30
Address: 60-64 Kings Road
Brighton BN1 1NA, UK
Phone: +44 1273 731330

#113
Sri India
Cuisines: Indian, Pakistani
Average price: $11-30
Address: 1-2 Wilmington Parade
Brighton BN1 8JJ, UK
Phone: +44 1273 330222

#114
Pinocchio
Cuisines: Italian, Pizza
Average price: Under $10
Address: 22 New Road
Brighton BN1 1UF, UK
Phone: +44 1273 677676

#115
Dover Castle
Cuisines: Pub, Seafood
Average price: $31-60
Address: 43 Southover Street
Brighton BN2 9UE, UK
Phone: +44 1273 245338

#116
Bhindis
Cuisines: Indian, Fast Food
Average price: $11-30
Address: 166 Lewes Road
Brighton BN2 3LD, UK
Phone: +44 1273 690390

#117
Madame Geisha
Cuisines: Asian Fusion, Nightclub
Average price: $11-30
Address: 75 - 79 East St
Brighton BN1 1NF, UK
Phone: +44 1273 770847

#118
Dumb Waiter
Cuisines: Breakfast & Brunch
Average price: $31-60
Address: 28 Sydney Street
Brighton BN1 4EP, UK
Phone: +44 1273 602526

#119
Misty's
Cuisines: British, Lounge
Average price: $31-60
Address: 116 Church Rd
Brighton BN3 2EA, UK
Phone: +44 1273 220302

#120
The Signalman
Cuisines: Pub, GastroPub
Average price: $11-30
Address: 76 Ditchling Rise
Brighton BN1 4QQ, UK
Phone: +44 1273 689783

#121
Good Companions
Cuisines: Pub, GastroPub
Average price: Under $10
Address: 132 Dyke Road
Brighton BN1 3TE, UK
Phone: +44 1273 202062

#122
Bodega D Tapa
Cuisines: Tapas Bar
Average price: $11-30
Address: 111 Church St
Brighton BN1 1, UK
Phone: +44 1273 674116

#123
Park View
Cuisines: Pub, British
Average price: $11-30
Address: 71 Preston Drove
Brighton BN1 6LD, UK
Phone: +44 1273 541663

#124
Genghis Khans Mongollan Barbecue
Cuisines: Chinese
Average price: $11-30
Address: 15-17 Middle St
Brighton BN1 1AL, UK
Phone: +44 1273 323605

#125
TFI Lunch
Cuisines: Breakfast & Brunch, Sandwiches, Coffee & Tea
Average price: Under $10
Address: 56 Queens Road
Brighton BN1 3XD, UK
Phone: +44 1273 720017

#126
La Fourchette
Cuisines: Breakfast & Brunch, French
Average price: $11-30
Address: 42 Church Rd
Brighton BN3 2FN, UK
Phone: +44 1273 733228

#127
Grand Central
Cuisines: Pub, GastroPub
Average price: $11-30
Address: 29-30 Surrey Street
Brighton BN1 3PA, UK
Phone: +44 1273 329086

#128
Al Rouche
Cuisines: Mediterranean
Average price: Under $10
Address: 44 Preston St
Brighton BN1 2HP, UK
Phone: +44 1273 734810

#129
Good Friends
Cuisines: Chinese
Average price: $11-30
Address: 24-25 Preston Street
Brighton BN1 2HN, UK
Phone: +44 1273 779836

#130
The Arrogant Frog Brasserie
Cuisines: French
Average price: Above $61
Address: 64 Kings Road
Brighton BN1 1NA, UK
Phone: +44 1273 721488

#131
Buddys
Cuisines: Fish & Chips
Average price: $11-30
Address: 50 Kings Road
Brighton BN1 1NA, UK
Phone: +44 1273 220313

#132
Chilka House
Cuisines: Chinese
Average price: $11-30
Address: 15 Baker Street
Brighton BN1 4JN, UK
Phone: +44 1273 677085

#133
MEATliquor Brighton
Cuisines: American, Burgers
Average price: $11-30
Address: 22-23 York Place
Brighton BN1 4GU, UK
Phone: +44 1273 917710

#134
JB's American Diner
Cuisines: American
Average price: $11-30
Address: 31 Kings Road
Brighton BN1 1NR, UK
Phone: +44 1273 771776

#135
Sofias
Cuisines: Italian
Average price: Under $10
Address: 24 Ship St
Brighton BN1 1AD, UK
Phone: +44 1273 321233

#136
New Lotus
Cuisines: Fast Food, Chinese
Average price: $31-60
Address: 107 Dyke Road
Brighton BN1 3JE, UK
Phone: +44 1273 326336

#137
Murasaki Bento
Cuisines: Sushi Bar
Average price: $11-30
Address: 16 Montpelier Place
Brighton BN1 3BF, UK
Phone: +44 1273 775771

#138
Blackbird Tea Rooms
Cuisines: Tea Rooms, Coffee & Tea
Average price: $11-30
Address: 30 Ship Street
Brighton BN1 1AD, UK
Phone: +44 1273 249454

#139
Wild Cherry
Cuisines: Delis, Coffee & Tea
Average price: $11-30
Address: 91 Queens Park Road
Brighton BN2 0GJ, UK
Phone: +44 1273 691494

#140
Los Taquitos
Cuisines: Mexican, Fast Food
Average price: Under $10
Address: 6 York Place
Brighton BN1 4GU, UK
Phone: +44 1273 628630

#141
Inside Out
Cuisines: Breakfast & Brunch
Average price: $11-30
Address: 95 Gloucester Rd
Brighton BN1 4AP, UK
Phone: +44 1273 692912

#142
Mad Hatter Cafe
Cuisines: Coffee & Tea, Breakfast & Brunch, Juice Bar & Smoothies
Average price: Under $10
Address: 35 Montpelier Rd
Brighton BN1 3BA, UK
Phone: +44 1273 722279

#143
Bankers Restaurant
Cuisines: Fish & Chips, Seafood
Average price: $11-30
Address: 116a Western Road
Brighton BN1 2AB, UK
Phone: +44 1273 328267

#144
Lovefit Cafe
Cuisines: Juice Bar & Smoothies, Coffee & Tea, Breakfast & Brunch
Average price: $31-60
Address: 14 Brighton Sq
Brighton BN1 1HD, UK
Phone: +44 1273 777941

#145
Coast to Coast
Cuisines: American
Average price: $31-60
Address: Brighton Marina
Brighton BN2 5WA, UK
Phone: +44 1273 626170

#146
The Hampton
Cuisines: Pub, GastroPub
Average price: $11-30
Address: 57 Upper North St
Brighton BN1 3FH, UK
Phone: +44 1273 731347

#147
Fat Leo
Cuisines: Italian, Pizza
Average price: $11-30
Address: 16 Market Street
Brighton BN1 1HH, UK
Phone: +44 1273 325135

#148
Pizza & Pasta Brasserie
Cuisines: Italian
Average price: $11-30
Address: 49 St James's Street
Brighton BN2 1RG, UK
Phone: +44 1273 604060

#149
Casalingo
Cuisines: Italian, Seafood
Average price: Under $10
Address: 29 Preston Street
Brighton BN1 2HP, UK
Phone: +44 1273 328775

#150
The Station Pub
Cuisines: Bar, Pizza
Average price: $31-60
Address: 100 Goldstone Villas
Brighton BN3 3RU, UK
Phone: +44 1273 733660

#151
Brighton Bystander
Cuisines: Breakfast & Brunch
Average price: $31-60
Address: 1 Terminus Road
Brighton BN1 3PD, UK
Phone: +44 1273 329364

#152
Kambi's Restaurant
Cuisines: Middle Eastern
Average price: $11-30
Address: 107 Western Road
Brighton BN1 2AA, UK
Phone: +44 1273 327934

#153
Giggling Squid
Cuisines: Thai
Average price: $11-30
Address: 11 Market St
Brighton BN1 1HH, UK
Phone: +44 1273 737373

#154
Costa Coffee
Cuisines: Coffee & Tea, Sandwiches
Average price: $11-30
Address: 32 Bond Street
Brighton BN1 1, UK
Phone: +44 1273 772024

#155
Bella Napoli
Cuisines: Italian
Average price: $11-30
Address: 19 Waterfront
Brighton BN2 5WA, UK
Phone: +44 1273 818577

#156
Okinami
Cuisines: Japanese, Sushi Bar
Average price: $31-60
Address: 6 New Road
Brighton BN1 1UF, UK
Phone: +44 1273 773777

#157
Caffe Aldo
Cuisines: Italian, Coffee & Tea
Average price: Under $10
Address: 77 Trafalgar Street
Brighton BN1 4EB, UK
Phone: +44 1273 819181

#158
Pizza King
Cuisines: Fast Food, Pizza
Average price: $11-30
Address: 56 Preston Street
Brighton BN1 2HE, UK
Phone: +44 1273 737272

#159
The Coal Shed
Cuisines: Barbeque
Average price: Above $61
Address: 8 Boyces Street
Brighton BN1 1AN, UK
Phone: +44 1273 322998

#160
Aberdeen Steak House
Cuisines: British
Average price: $11-30
Address: 27-28 Preston Street
Brighton BN1 2HP, UK
Phone: +44 1273 326892

#161
Cafe Motu
Cuisines: Breakfast & Brunch
Average price: Under $10
Address: 6 Trafalgar St
Brighton BN1 4EQ, UK
Phone: +44 1273 709655

#162
Pizza King
Cuisines: Fast Food
Average price: Under $10
Address: 42 Kings Road
Brighton BN1 1NA, UK
Phone: +44 1273 725225

#163
Chopstick Express
Cuisines: Fast Food
Average price: Above $61
Address: 28 Baker Street
Brighton BN1 4JN, UK
Phone: +44 1273 609408

#164
The Hartington
Cuisines: Pub, GastroPub
Average price: $11-30
Address: 41 Whippingham Road
Brighton BN2 3PF, UK
Phone: +44 1273 682874

#165
The Brasserie
Cuisines: Italian, Bar
Average price: $11-30
Address: 15d The Village Square Shop
Brighton BN2 5WA, UK
Phone: +44 1273 818026

#166
Sing-Li Fish Chips
Cuisines: Seafood
Average price: Under $10
Address: 39 Guildford Road
Brighton BN1 3LW, UK
Phone: +44 1273 328686

#167
Pizza 7
Cuisines: Pizza
Average price: $11-30
Address: 60 Ship Street
Brighton BN1 1AE, UK
Phone: +44 1273 327756

#168
Blind Lemon Alley
Cuisines: American, Tex-Mex, Mexican
Average price: $11-30
Address: 41 Middle St
Brighton BN1 1AL, UK
Phone: +44 1273 205151

#169
La Marinade
Cuisines: French, European
Average price: $31-60
Address: 77 St Georges Road
Brighton BN2 1EF, UK
Phone: +44 1273 600992

#170
Aguadulce
Cuisines: Spanish, Tapas Bar
Average price: $11-30
Address: 10-11 King's Road
Brighton BN1 1NE, UK
Phone: +44 1273 328672

#171
Ottoman Shisha Bar
Cuisines: Turkish, Hookah Bar
Average price: $11-30
Address: 35-38 Lewes Road
Brighton BN2 3HQ, UK
Phone: +44 1273 605314

#172
Mumbai Express
Cuisines: Indian
Average price: $11-30
Address: 17 sutherland rd
Brighton BN2 0EQ, UK
Phone: +44 1273 676005

#173
Burger King
Cuisines: American, Burgers, Fast Food
Average price: $11-30
Address: 63-65 North Street
Brighton BN1 1RH, UK
Phone: +44 1273 325466

#174
Mo:Mo Dumpling Bar
Cuisines: Tea Rooms
Average price: $11-30
Address: 15A Kensington Gardens
Brighton BN1 4AL, UK
Phone: +44 1273 698129

#175
The Cornerstone
Cuisines: Pub, Caribbean
Average price: Under $10
Address: 2-6 Elm Grove
Brighton BN2 3DD, UK
Phone: +44 1273 691028

#176
Lucky Star
Cuisines: Chinese, Buffet
Average price: Under $10
Address: 101 Trafalgar Street
Brighton BN1 4ER, UK
Phone: +44 1273 687064

#177
Jade
Cuisines: Chinese, Japanese
Average price: $11-30
Address: 29 Western Rd
Brighton BN3 1AF, UK
Phone: +44 1273 778180

#178
Buffet Island
Cuisines: Chinese, Buffet
Average price: $11-30
Address: 18 York Place
Brighton BN1 4GU, UK
Phone: +44 1273 698606

#179
AA Charcoal Grill
Cuisines: Turkish, Barbeque
Average price: Under $10
Address: 41 Lewes Rd
Brighton BN2 3HQ, UK
Phone: +44 1273 571003

#180
Saint James
Cuisines: Pub, Thai
Average price: $11-30
Address: 16 Madeira Place
Brighton BN2 1TN, UK
Phone: +44 1273 626696

#181
McDonald's
Cuisines: Fast Food
Average price: Above $61
Address: Brighton Marina Village
Brighton BN2 5UT, UK
Phone: +44 1273 819111

#182
Oxygen
Cuisines: Lounge, Burgers
Average price: Under $10
Address: 74 West St
Brighton BN1 2RA, UK
Phone: +44 1273 727378

#183
Bath Arms
Cuisines: Pub, British, Coffee & Tea
Average price: $11-30
Address: 4 Meeting House Lane
Brighton BN1 1HB, UK
Phone: +44 1273 731864

#184
Forfars Fresh
Cuisines: Bakery, Sandwiches
Average price: Under $10
Address: 12a Imperial Arcade
Brighton BN1 3EA, UK
Phone: +44 1273 325807

#185
Caffe Nero
Cuisines: Coffee & Tea, Sandwiches
Average price: $11-30
Address: 39-40 Bond St
Brighton BN1 1RD, UK
Phone: +44 1273 723912

#186
Efes Kebab
Cuisines: Fast Food
Average price: Under $10
Address: 53 Preston St
Brighton BN1 2HE, UK
Phone: +44 1273 205133

#187
Poppy's Sandwich Bar
Cuisines: Coffee & Tea, Sandwiches
Average price: Under $10
Address: 58a London Road
Brighton BN1 4JE, UK
Phone: +44 1273 672235

#188
Twisted Lemon
Cuisines: Cocktail Bar, British
Average price: Under $10
Address: 41 Middle St
Brighton BN1 1AL, UK
Phone: +44 1273 726693

#189
King & Queen
Cuisines: Pub, British, Sports Bar
Average price: Under $10
Address: 13-17 Marlborough Place
Brighton BN1 1UB, UK
Phone: +44 1273 607207

#190
Tuckers
Cuisines: Fast Food
Average price: $11-30
Address: 100 ST. Georges Road
Brighton BN2 1EA, UK
Phone: +44 1273 692452

#191
Nishat Tandoori
Cuisines: Indian, Fast Food
Average price: $11-30
Address: 58 Preston St
Brighton BN1 2, UK
Phone: +44 1273 321701

#192
Pizza Express
Cuisines: Italian, Pizza
Average price: $11-30
Address: Jubilee Street
Brighton BN1 1GE, UK
Phone: +44 1273 697691

#193
Bella Italia Restaurant
Cuisines: Italian
Average price: $11-30
Address: 24 Market Street
Brighton BN1 1HH, UK
Phone: +44 1273 777607

#194
Beach House Cafe
Cuisines: Sandwiches, Coffee & Tea
Average price: Under $10
Address: 21 King's Road Arches
Brighton BN1 2LN, UK
Phone: +44 872 148 6446

#195
China Garden
Cuisines: Chinese
Average price: $31-60
Address: 24 Preston Road
Brighton BN1 4QF, UK
Phone: +44 1273 696900

#196
The Gossip Cafe
Cuisines: Coffee & Tea
Average price: $11-30
Address: 57 St James's St
Brighton BN2 1QG, UK
Phone: +44 7796 867785

#197
Darcy's Restaurant
Cuisines: Seafood, British
Average price: $31-60
Address: 49 Market Street
Brighton BN1 1HH, UK
Phone: +44 1273 325560

#198
Strada
Cuisines: Italian, Pizza
Average price: $11-30
Address: 160-161 North Street
Brighton BN1 1EZ, UK
Phone: +44 1273 202070

#199
Subway
Cuisines: Sandwiches
Average price: Under $10
Address: 134 London Road
Brighton BN1 4JH, UK
Phone: +44 1273 628941

#200
Thai Pad Thai
Cuisines: Thai
Average price: Under $10
Address: 72 Dyke Road
Brighton BN1 7JD, UK
Phone: +44 1273 737878

#201
Pizza Express Restaurant
Cuisines: Pizza
Average price: $11-30
Address: 36 Ship Street
Brighton BN1 1AB, UK
Phone: +44 1895 618618

#202
Lydea
Cuisines: Vegetarian
Average price: $11-30
Address: 105 Western Road
Brighton BN1 2AA, UK
Phone: +44 1273 965904

#203
Grubbs Diner
Cuisines: Fast Food
Average price: Under $10
Address: 27 York Place
Brighton BN1 4GU, UK
Phone: +44 1273 697226

#204
The Buccaneer
Cuisines: Breakfast & Brunch
Average price: Under $10
Address: 186 Kings Road Arches
Brighton BN1 1NB, UK
Phone: +44 1273 321393

#205
Tookta's Cafe
Cuisines: Thai
Average price: $11-30
Address: 30 Spring St
Brighton BN1 3EF, UK
Phone: +44 1273 748071

#206
Cote
Cuisines: French
Average price: $31-60
Address: 115-116 Church Street
Brighton BN1 1UP, UK
Phone: +44 1273 687541

#207
Las Tortas
Cuisines: Italian
Average price: Under $10
Address: 48 Norfolk Square
Brighton BN1 2PA, UK
Phone: +44 1273 737222

#208
Carlito Burrito
Cuisines: Street Vendor
Average price: $11-30
Address: 12 York Place
Brighton BN1 4GU, UK
Phone: +44 1273 671191

#209
Chez Dimitrina
Cuisines: Coffee & Tea, French
Average price: Under $10
Address: 16 Sydney St
Brighton BN1 4EN, UK
Phone: +44 1273 625222

#210
Seagull Restaurant
Cuisines: Seafood
Average price: $11-30
Address: 11-12 Madeira Dr
Brighton BN2 1PS, UK
Phone: +44 1273 604462

#211
The Meeting Place
Cuisines: Breakfast & Brunch
Average price: Under $10
Address: Kings Road
Brighton BN1 2, UK
Phone: +44 1273 206417

#212
Seven Dials
Cuisines: British
Average price: $31-60
Address: 1 Buckingham Place
Brighton BN3 1UH, UK
Phone: +44 1273 701222

#213
Pizza Me A Slice For You
Cuisines: Pizza
Average price: Under $10
Address: The Kiosk Elm Grove
Brighton BN2, UK
Phone: +44 1273 622210

#214
Oriental Takeaway
Cuisines: Fast Food, Chinese
Average price: $11-30
Address: 70 Lewes Road
Brighton BN2 3HZ, UK
Phone: +44 1273 683543

#215
Ganges
Cuisines: Indian, Lounge
Average price: $11-30
Address: 93 Church Rd
Brighton BN3 2BA, UK
Phone: +44 1273 728292

#216
Old Orleans
Cuisines: American, Cajun/Creole
Average price: $11-30
Address: 1-3 Prince Albert Street
Brighton BN1 1HE, UK
Phone: +44 1273 747000

#217
The Iron Duke
Cuisines: Pub, Guest House, British
Average price: $11-30
Address: 3 Waterloo Street
Brighton BN3 1AQ, UK
Phone: +44 1273 734806

#218
The Stoneham
Cuisines: Pub, Pizza
Average price: Above $61
Address: 153 Portland Road
Brighton BN3, UK
Phone: +44 1273 383840

#219
All Bar One
Cuisines: Wine Bar, British
Average price: $11-30
Address: 2-3 Pavilion Bldg
Brighton BN1 1EE, UK
Phone: +44 1273 207593

#220
Subway
Cuisines: Sandwiches
Average price: Under $10
Address: 109 Queens Road
Brighton BN1 3XF, UK
Phone: +44 1273 722333

#221
GFC
Cuisines: Fast Food
Average price: $11-30
Address: 22 Church Rd
Brighton BN3 2FN, UK
Phone: +44 1273 749490

#222
Mr Noodles
Cuisines: Japanese
Average price: Under $10
Address: 35 Queens Road
Brighton BN1 3XB, UK
Phone: +44 1273 733999

#223
Al Nakhl
Cuisines: Turkish
Average price: Above $61
Address: 48 West Street
Brighton BN1 2RA, UK
Phone: +44 1273 732832

#224
Burger King
Cuisines: American, Burgers, Fast Food
Average price: Under $10
Address: Madeira Drive
Brighton BN2 1TB, UK
Phone: +44 1273 609029

#225
Cafe Arcadia
Cuisines: Breakfast & Brunch
Average price: $11-30
Address: 7 Dyke Rd
Brighton BN1 3FE, UK
Phone: +44 1273 326600

#226
GNC
Cuisines: Delis
Average price: $31-60
Address: Churchill Square
Brighton BN1 2TD, UK
Phone: +44 1273 710150

#227
Wokmania
Cuisines: Chinese, Vegetarian
Average price: $31-60
Address: Unit 1 Avalon 65 West Street
Brighton BN1 2RA, UK
Phone: +44 1273 746294

#228
Subway
Cuisines: Sandwiches
Average price: Under $10
Address: 146 North Street
Brighton BN1 1RE, UK
Phone: +44 1273 236059

#229
Breakfast at Tiffany's
Cuisines: Coffee & Tea,
Breakfast & Brunch, British
Average price: Under $10
Address: 22 North Rd
Brighton BN1 1YA, UK
Phone: +44 1273 674209

#230
Coffee Republic UK
Cuisines: Coffee & Tea
Average price: $31-60
Address: 54 Western Road
Brighton BN1 2EB, UK
Phone: +44 1273 730550

#231
Bella
Cuisines: Italian, Coffee & Tea
Average price: $11-30
Address: 120 St James St
Brighton BN2 1TH, UK
Phone: +44 1273 623485

#232
China Town 2
Cuisines: Chinese, Fast Food
Average price: Under $10
Address: 94 Upper Lewes Rd
Brighton BN2 3FE, UK
Phone: +44 1273 380850

#233
Swallow House
Cuisines: Chinese, Fast Food
Average price: Under $10
Address: 3 Lewes Rd
Brighton BN2 3HP, UK
Phone: +44 1273 692794

#234
The Brasserie Fish
Cuisines: Seafood
Average price: $11-30
Address: 3a Waterfront
Brighton BN2 5WA, UK
Phone: +44 1273 698989

#235
Katarina Harvester
Cuisines: British, Pub
Average price: $11-30
Address: Village Square
Brighton BN2 5WD, UK
Phone: +44 1273 606268

#236
**The Gourmet
Fish and Chip Company**
Cuisines: Coffee & Tea, Fish & Chips
Average price: Under $10
Address: 18 Waterfront
Brighton BN2 5WA, UK
Phone: +44 1273 670701

#237
Strada - Brighton Marina
Cuisines: Italian
Average price: $31-60
Address: Brighton Marina
Brighton BN2 5WA, UK
Phone: +44 1273 686821

#238
Italian Delicatessen
Cuisines: Delis, Coffee & Tea
Average price: $11-30
Address: 92 Dyke Road
Brighton BN1 3JD, UK
Phone: +44 1273 326147

#239
The Prince Arthur
Cuisines: Pub, British
Average price: $11-30
Address: 38 Dean Street
Brighton BN1 3EG, UK
Phone: +44 1273 205797

#240
Kokoro
Cuisines: Sushi Bar
Average price: Under $10
Address: 57 North Street
Brighton BN1 1RH, UK
Phone: +44 1273 771292

#241
Aysha Tandoori
Cuisines: Indian, Pakistani
Average price: Under $10
Address: 7 Oxford St
Brighton BN1 4LA, UK
Phone: +44 1273 608885

#242
Zizzi
Cuisines: Italian, Pizza
Average price: $11-30
Address: 7-8 Prince Albert Street
Brighton BN1 1HE, UK
Phone: +44 1273 323273

#243
Pomegranate
Cuisines: Middle Eastern
Average price: $11-30
Address: 10 Manchester Street
Brighton BN2 1TF, UK
Phone: +44 1273 628386

#244
Pret a Manger
Cuisines: Coffee & Tea, Sandwiches
Average price: Under $10
Address: 35 East St
Brighton BN1 1HL, UK
Phone: +44 20 7932 5397

#245
Gourmet Burger Kitchen
Cuisines: American, Burgers
Average price: $11-30
Address: 44-47 Gardner Street
Brighton BN1 1UN, UK
Phone: +44 1273 685895

#246
Costa Coffee
Cuisines: Coffee & Tea, Sandwiches
Average price: $11-30
Address: 2 Dyke Rd
Brighton BN1 3FE, UK
Phone: +44 1273 725124

#247
La Choza
Cuisines: Mexican
Average price: Under $10
Address: 36 Gloucester Road
Brighton BN1 4AP, UK
Phone: +44 1273 945926

#248
Me Old China
Cuisines: Fast Food, Chinese, Buffet
Average price: Under $10
Address: 46 West Street
Brighton BN1 2RA, UK
Phone: +44 1273 711518

#249
Street Thai
Cuisines: Thai
Average price: $11-30
Address: 20 Brighton Square
Brighton BN1 1HD, UK
Phone: +44 1273 207444

#250
Caffe Nero
Cuisines: Coffee & Tea, Sandwiches
Average price: $11-30
Address: 16 Prince Albert St
Brighton BN1 1HF, UK
Phone: +44 1273 727726

#251
Cafe Laziz
Cuisines: British, Sandwiches
Average price: $11-30
Address: 48 Gardner Street
Brighton BN1 1UN, UK
Phone: +44 1273 625544

#252
The Dip Cafe
Cuisines: Breakfast & Brunch
Average price: $11-30
Address: 5 Hollingbury Place
Brighton BN1 7GE, UK
Phone: +44 1273 563605

#253
Rocky's
Cuisines: Fast Food
Average price: $11-30
Address: 147 Edward Street
Brighton BN2 0JG, UK
Phone: +44 1273 687689

#254
Square Bar-Restaurant
Cuisines: Wine Bar, Lounge, Italian
Average price: $11-30
Address: 79 Western Road
Brighton BN3 2JQ, UK
Phone: +44 1273 772777

#255
Lee's Garden
Cuisines: Fast Food, Chinese
Average price: Under $10
Address: 186 Lewes Road
Brighton BN2 3LD, UK
Phone: +44 1273 600138

#256
Jenny's Fish & Chips
Cuisines: Fish & Chips, Fast Food
Average price: Under $10
Address: 86 Preston Drove
Brighton BN1 6LB, UK
Phone: +44 1273 881700

#257
Karma
Cuisines: Pub, British
Average price: $11-30
Address: 5 Waterfront
Brighton BN2 5WA, UK
Phone: +44 1273 818000

#258
Bellota Bar Y Tapas
Cuisines: Spanish, Tapas Bar
Average price: $11-30
Address: 165 North Street
Brighton BN1 1EA, UK
Phone: +44 1273 737342

#259
Wagamama
Cuisines: Japanese
Average price: $11-30
Address: 30 Kensington Street
Brighton BN41 2HD, UK
Phone: +44 1273 688892

#260
Lovefit Cafe
Cuisines: Coffee & Tea, Breakfast & Brunch, Juice Bar & Smoothies
Average price: $11-30
Address: 110 Queens Road
Brighton BN1 3XF, UK
Phone: +44 1273 720100

#261
Sea Haze
Cuisines: Seafood Markets
Average price: Under $10
Address: 207 Kings Road
Brighton BN1 1NB, UK
Phone: +44 1273 777007

#262
Time Out Cafe
Cuisines: Cafe, Breakfast & Brunch
Average price: Under $10
Address: 3-4 East Street
Brighton BN1 1HP, UK
Phone: +44 1273 777312

#263
Destination 100
Cuisines: Diners
Average price: Under $10
Address: 100 St. James St
Brighton BN2 1TP, UK
Phone: +44 1273 606030

#264
Capers
Cuisines: Coffee & Tea, British
Average price: $11-30
Address: 27 Gardner Street
Brighton BN1 1UP, UK
Phone: +44 1273 675550

#265
Fraser's Sandwich Station
Cuisines: Coffee & Tea, Sandwiches
Average price: Under $10
Address: 1A Castle Sq
Brighton BN1 1EG, UK
Phone: +44 1273 202067

#266
KFC
Cuisines: Fast Food
Average price: Under $10
Address: 63-65 Western Road
Brighton BN1 2HA, UK
Phone: +44 1273 328821

#267
Pasha
Cuisines: Seafood, Bar
Average price: Under $10
Address: 62 West Street
Brighton BN1 2RA, UK
Phone: +44 1273 771010

#268
Mac's Cafe
Cuisines: Breakfast & Brunch, British
Average price: $11-30
Address: 30 Arundel Road
Brighton BN2 5TD, UK
Phone: +44 1273 692621

#269
Hasina Tandoori
Cuisines: Fast Food
Average price: $11-30
Address: 92 Preston Drove
Brighton BN1 6LB, UK
Phone: +44 1273 542626

#270
Joeies Takeaway
Cuisines: Pizza, Fast Food
Average price: Under $10
Address: 32 Viaduct Rd
Brighton BN1 4NB, UK
Phone: +44 1273 708080

#271
La Florentina
Cuisines: Italian, Portuguese
Average price: $11-30
Address: 50 Norfolk Square
Brighton BN1 2PA, UK
Phone: +44 1273 774049

#272
Divalls Cafe
Cuisines: Coffee & Tea,
Breakfast & Brunch
Average price: Under $10
Address: 3 Terminus Road
Brighton BN1 3PD, UK
Phone: +44 1273 776277

#273
Tortilla
Cuisines: Mexican, Fast Food
Average price: Under $10
Address: 37 West Street
Brighton BN1 2RE, UK
Phone: +44 1273 748069

#274
Magic Wok
Cuisines: Fast Food, Chinese
Average price: $11-30
Address: 49 Preston St
Brighton BN1 2HP, UK
Phone: +44 1273 327788

#275
Costa Coffee
Cuisines: Coffee & Tea,
Breakfast & Brunch, Sandwiches
Average price: $11-30
Address: 17 London Road
Brighton BN1 4JA, UK
Phone: +44 1273 604646

#276
Brighton Wok
Cuisines: Fast Food, Chinese
Average price: $11-30
Address: 34 New England Road
Brighton BN1 4GG, UK
Phone: +44 1273 270490

#277
The Eagle
Cuisines: Pub, British
Average price: $11-30
Address: 125 Gloucester Road
Brighton BN1 4AF, UK
Phone: +44 1273 607765

#278
Loving Hut
Cuisines: Vegan
Average price: Under $10
Address: The Level St Peter's Place
Brighton BN1 4SA, UK
Phone: +44 1273 689532

#279
Agra Balti House
Cuisines: Indian, Pakistani
Average price: $11-30
Address: 60 Ship St
Brighton BN1 1AE, UK
Phone: +44 1273 324384

#280
Pizza Hut
Cuisines: Pizza, Fast Food
Average price: $11-30
Address: 132 - 135 Lewes Rd
Brighton BN2 3LG, UK
Phone: +44 1273 670670

#281
Green Tomato
Cuisines: Coffee & Tea, Sandwiches
Average price: $11-30
Address: 100a Western Rd
Brighton BN1 2AA, UK
Phone: +44 1273 727285

#282
Friends Fish and Chips
Cuisines: Fish & Chips
Average price: Under $10
Address: 67 queens road
Brighton BN1 3XD, UK
Phone: +44 1273 243665

#283
Izzy Café
Cuisines: Diners, Breakfast & Brunch
Average price: Under $10
Address: 2 St James's St
Brighton BN1 1RE, UK
Phone: +44 1273 671908

#284
Pavilion Gardens Cafe
Cuisines: Sandwiches, Desserts
Average price: Under $10
Address: New Road
Brighton BN1 1UG, UK
Phone: +44 1273 730712

#285
Cheeky Chicken
Cuisines: Fast Food
Average price: Under $10
Address: 59 Preston Street
Brighton BN1 2HE, UK
Phone: +44 1273 822888

#286
Yates
Cuisines: Pub, Nightclub, British
Average price: Under $10
Address: 59 W Street
Brighton BN1 2RA, UK
Phone: +44 1273 731117

#287
Riz Raz
Cuisines: Hookah Bar, African
Average price: $11-30
Address: 8 Western Road
Brighton BN3 1AE, UK
Phone: +44 1273 777971

#288
Relax Cafe
Cuisines: Coffee & Tea, Sandwiches
Average price: Under $10
Address: 50 Preston Road
Brighton BN1 4QF, UK
Phone: +44 1273 818828

#289
McDonald's
Cuisines: Fast Food
Average price: Under $10
Address: Unit A Churchill Square
Brighton BN1 2TE, UK
Phone: +44 1273 747924

#290
Master Mariner
Cuisines: Pub, British
Average price: $11-30
Address: Village Square
Brighton BN2 5WD, UK
Phone: +44 1273 818563

#291
Pizza Hut
Cuisines: Pizza, Fast Food
Average price: $11-30
Address: 2 Dyke Road
Brighton BN1 3FE, UK
Phone: +44 1273 328666

#292
China Chef Express
Cuisines: Chinese, Fast Food
Average price: Under $10
Address: 15 Beaconsfield Road
Brighton BN1 4QH, UK
Phone: +44 1273 688290

#293
Delight Kebab
Cuisines: Turkish
Average price: $31-60
Address: 15 Preston Road
Brighton BN1 4QE, UK
Phone: +44 1273 695508

#294
Friends
Cuisines: Fast Food
Average price: Under $10
Address: 67 Queen's Rd
Brighton BN1 3XD, UK
Phone: +44 1273 772330

#295
The Cow
Cuisines: Pub, British
Average price: $11-30
Address: 95/97 Dyke Road
Brighton BN1 3JE, UK
Phone: +44 1273 772370

#296
The Blue Man
Cuisines: African, Moroccan
Average price: $11-30
Address: 8 Queens Road
Brighton BN1 3WA, UK
Phone: +44 1273 726003

#297
Bucket & Spade Beach Cafe
Cuisines: British, Coffee & Tea, Breakfast & Brunch
Average price: $11-30
Address: 28 Kings Rd Arches
Brighton BN1 2LN, UK
Phone: +44 1273 220222

#298
Sobs Takeaway
Cuisines: Fast Food
Average price: $11-30
Address: 16 Montpelier Place
Brighton BN1 3BF, UK
Phone: +44 1273 729082

#299
P C Pickles
Cuisines: Fast Food
Average price: Under $10
Address: 3-6 Francis Street
Brighton BN1 4JT, UK
Phone: +44 1273 622113

#300
Papa John's Pizza Brighton
Cuisines: Pizza
Average price: $11-30
Address: 13 Preston Road
Brighton BN1 4, UK
Phone: +44 1273 607080

#301
Curry Hut
Cuisines: Fast Food, Indian
Average price: Under $10
Address: 162 Edward Street
Brighton BN2 0JB, UK
Phone: +44 1273 609349

#302
Terraces Bar and Grill
Cuisines: Mediterranean, British
Average price: $11-30
Address: Marine Parade
Brighton BN2, UK
Phone: +44 1273 570526

#303
Anatolia Cuisine
Cuisines: Caterers, Turkish
Average price: Under $10
Address: 51 St James Street
Brighton BN2 1QG, UK
Phone: +44 1273 693467

#304
Eshnas Nutrition Indian Takeaway
Cuisines: Fast Food, Indian
Average price: $11-30
Address: 4 Coombe Terrace
Brighton BN2 4AD, UK
Phone: +44 1273 570606

#305
Marions
Cuisines: Breakfast & Brunch, British
Average price: $11-30
Address: 3 Beaconsfield Parade
Brighton BN1 6DN, UK
Phone: +44 1273 556526

#306
Lodestar Cafe
Cuisines: Sandwiches, Breakfast & Brunch
Average price: $11-30
Address: 163 Kings Road Arches
Brighton BN1 1NB, UK
Phone: +44 7973 296514

#307
Out To Lunch
Cuisines: Fast Food, Sandwiches
Average price: Under $10
Address: 8 Preston Road
Brighton BN1 4QF, UK
Phone: +44 1273 694390

#308
Model Fish Fryer
Cuisines: Fish & Chips
Average price: Under $10
Address: 136 Preston Drove
Brighton BN1 6FJ, UK
Phone: +44 1273 503871

#309
All Nite Diner
Cuisines: Diners
Average price: $31-60
Address: 19-21 Market Street
Brighton BN2 9QF, UK
Phone: +44 1273 608273

#310
Kebab Knight
Cuisines: Fast Food
Average price: $11-30
Address: 15 Coombe Terrace
Brighton BN2 4AD, UK
Phone: +44 1273 690771

#311
China Kitchen
Cuisines: Fast Food
Average price: Under $10
Address: 17 Coombe Terrace Lewes Road
Brighton BN2 4AD, UK
Phone: +44 1273 680894

#312
China China
Cuisines: Chinese
Average price: Under $10
Address: 33-35 Preston Street
Brighton BN1 2HP, UK
Phone: +44 1273 328028

#313
The Office
Cuisines: Pub, Thai
Average price: $31-60
Address: 8-9 Sydney Street
Brighton BN1 4EN, UK
Phone: +44 1273 609134

#314
Dial A Pizza
Cuisines: Fast Food
Average price: $11-30
Address: 103 Dyke Road
Brighton BN1 3JE, UK
Phone: +44 1273 220021

#315
Cummin Up
Cuisines: Caribbean
Average price: Under $10
Address: 2 Preston Circus
Brighton BN1 4JQ, UK
Phone: +44 1273 679000

#316
Pizza Di Roma
Cuisines: Fast Food, Halal
Average price: Under $10
Address: 51 Lewes Road
Brighton BN2 3HW, UK
Phone: +44 1273 626233

#317
Pizzaiola Pizza
Cuisines: Pizza
Average price: Under $10
Address: 76 Islingword Road
Brighton BN2 9SL, UK
Phone: +44 1273 684681

#318
The Trawlerman
Cuisines: Fish & Chips
Average price: Under $10
Address: 106 Gloucester Road
Brighton BN1 4AP, UK
Phone: +44 1273 681601

#319
Fiddler's Elbow
Cuisines: Irish, Pub
Average price: $11-30
Address: 11 Boyces Street
Brighton BN1 1AN, UK
Phone: +44 1273 325850

#320
Strada Restaurant
Cuisines: Italian
Average price: $11-30
Address: 3 Waterfront
Brighton BN2 5WA, UK
Phone: +44 1273 686821

#321
Kemp Town Chippy
Cuisines: Fish & Chips
Average price: Under $10
Address: 73 ST Georges Road
Brighton BN2 1EF, UK
Phone: +44 1273 680821

#322
Seven Bees Cafe
Cuisines: Breakfast & Brunch
Average price: Under $10
Address: 7b Ship Street Gardens
Brighton BN2 1ED, UK
Phone: +44 1273 279448

#323
Golden Fry
Cuisines: Fast Food, Fish & Chips
Average price: Under $10
Address: 2 Parade Valley Drive
Brighton BN1 5FG, UK
Phone: +44 1273 501444

#324
The Plaza
Cuisines: Italian
Average price: $11-30
Address: 43-45 Kings Road
Brighton BN1 1NA, UK
Phone: +44 1273 232222

#325
Nandos Chickenland
Cuisines: Portuguese
Average price: $11-30
Address: 34 Duke Street
Brighton BN1 1AG, UK
Phone: +44 1273 725483

#326
Jalalia Tandoori Takeaway
Cuisines: Indian
Average price: Under $10
Address: 31 Baker Street
Brighton BN1 4JN, UK
Phone: +44 1273 682288

#327
Um Elnour
Cuisines: Fast Food
Average price: Under $10
Address: 16 Western Road
Brighton BN3, UK
Phone: +44 1273 771478

#328
The Swan
Cuisines: British
Average price: $31-60
Address: No 9 Rock St
Brighton BN2 1NF, UK
Phone: +44 1273 606138

#329
The Courtyard
Cuisines: British
Average price: $11-30
Address: 20 New road
Brighton BN1, UK
Phone: +44 1273 819600

#330
Maharani Indian Takeaway
Cuisines: Fast Food
Average price: $11-30
Address: 52 Sillwood Street
Brighton BN1 2PS, UK
Phone: +44 1273 748001

#331
Dos Sombreros
Cuisines: Mexican
Average price: $11-30
Address: 24 Ship Street
Brighton BN1 1AD, UK
Phone: +44 1273 911455

#332
Otello Cafe
Cuisines: Coffee & Tea, Italian
Average price: $11-30
Address: 120 Church Rd
Brighton BN3 2AE, UK
Phone: +44 1273 729774

#333
Thai Spice Restaurant
Cuisines: Thai
Average price: Under $10
Address: 13 Boyces Street
Brighton BN1 1AN, UK
Phone: +44 1273 325195

#334
The Constant Service
Cuisines: Pub, British
Average price: $11-30
Address: 96 Islingword Rd
Brighton BN2 9, UK
Phone: +44 1273 607058

#335
The View
Cuisines: European, Seafood
Average price: $11-30
Address: Western Esplanade Kingsway
Brighton BN3 4FA, UK
Phone: +44 1273 207100

#336
Western Front
Cuisines: Pub, Social Club, British
Average price: Under $10
Address: 11 Cranbourne St
Brighton BN1 2RD, UK
Phone: +44 1273 725656

#337
Si Signore
Cuisines: Italian
Average price: $11-30
Address: 12 Sydney Street
Brighton BN1 4EN, UK
Phone: +44 1273 671266

#338
KFC
Cuisines: Fast Food
Average price: $11-30
Address: 22-23 London Road
Brighton BN1 4JB, UK
Phone: +44 1273 691598

#339
Pause Cafe
Cuisines: Coffee & Tea, Breakfast & Brunch
Average price: $11-30
Address: 1 Circus Parade
Brighton BN1 4GW, UK
Phone: +44 1273 690300

#340
Albion Kebabs
Cuisines: Mediterranean
Average price: Under $10
Address: 61 Queens Rd
Brighton BN1 3XD, UK
Phone: +44 1273 888860

#341
The Olive
Cuisines: Bistros
Average price: Under $10
Address: 19 Chatham Place
Brighton BN1, UK
Phone: +44 1273 640982

#342
Spencers Cafe
Cuisines: Cafe, Breakfast & Brunch
Average price: Under $10
Address: 95 St Georges Road
Brighton BN2 1EE, UK
Phone: +44 1273 840309

#343
LangeLee's
Cuisines: Coffee & Tea, British
Average price: $11-30
Address: 30 York Place
Brighton BN1 4, UK
Phone: +44 1273 684840

#344
Cous Cous House
Cuisines: Moroccan, Persian/Iranian
Average price: $11-30
Address: 10-11 Preston Street
Brighton BN1 2HN, UK
Phone: +44 1273 323230

#345
Casa Della Pizza
Cuisines: Italian
Average price: Under $10
Address: 27 North St
Brighton BN1 1EB, UK
Phone: +44 1273 205441

#346
Ground Coffee House
Cuisines: Coffee & Tea, Breakfast & Brunch
Average price: $11-30
Address: 36 St Georges Road
Brighton BN2 1ED, UK
Phone: +44 1273 696441

#347
Akash Tandoori
Cuisines: Indian, Pakistani
Average price: $11-30
Address: 26 Preston Street
Brighton BN1 2HN, UK
Phone: +44 1273 820213

#348
Little Budah
Cuisines: Thai
Average price: $11-30
Address: 72 Dyke Road
Brighton BN1 3JD, UK
Phone: +44 1273 737878

#349
Nashat Tandoori
Cuisines: Fast Food, Indian, Pakistani
Average price: $11-30
Address: 58 Preston Street
Brighton BN1 2HE, UK
Phone: +44 1273 321701

#350
Cala & Arrobas
Cuisines: Spanish
Average price: $11-30
Address: 42 Sydney Street
Brighton BN1 4EP, UK
Phone: +44 1273 673966

#351
Crepe Dentelle
Cuisines: Thai
Average price: $11-30
Address: 65 Preston Street
Brighton BN1 2HE, UK
Phone: +44 1273 323224

#352
Pablo's
Cuisines: Italian, Pizza
Average price: Under $10
Address: 36 Ship St
Brighton BN1 1AB, UK
Phone: +44 1273 208123

#353
Burger Off
Cuisines: Fast Food, Burgers
Average price: Under $10
Address: 52 Brunswick St West
Hove BN3 1EL, UK
Phone: +44 1273 326655

#354
Caroline Of Brunswick
Cuisines: Pub, British
Average price: Under $10
Address: 39 Ditchling Road
Brighton BN1 4SB, UK
Phone: +44 1273 624434

#355
The Pond
Cuisines: Thai, Pub
Average price: $11-30
Address: 49 Gloucester Road
Brighton BN1 4AQ, UK
Phone: +44 1273 621400

#356
The Townhouse
Cuisines: British
Average price: $11-30
Address: 81-82 St James Street
Brighton BN2 1PA, UK
Phone: +44 1273 693216

#357
Choys Chinese Restaurant
Cuisines: Chinese, American
Average price: $11-30
Address: 2-3 Little East Street
Brighton BN1 1HT, UK
Phone: +44 1273 325305

#358
Dave's Diner
Cuisines: Coffee & Tea, British
Average price: Under $10
Address: 87 Lewes Road
Brighton BN2 3HZ, UK
Phone: +44 1273 697696

#359
Nounou
Cuisines: Greek, African, Mediterranean
Average price: $31-60
Address: 120 ST. Georges Road
Brighton BN2 1EA, UK
Phone: +44 1273 682200

#360
Lucky Voice Karaoke
Cuisines: Karaoke, Bar, Pizza
Average price: $31-60
Address: 8 Black Lion Street
Brighton BN1 1ND, UK
Phone: +44 1273 715770

#361
Subway
Cuisines: Fast Food, Sandwiches
Average price: $11-30
Address: Eastern Road
Brighton BN2 5BE, UK
Phone: +44 7795 642240

#362
Tutti Frutti
Cuisines: Food, Italian
Average price: $11-30
Address: 92 Dyke Rd
Brighton BN1 3DJ, UK
Phone: +44 1273 326147

#363
Uncle Sams Hamburger Express
Cuisines: Fast Food, Burgers
Average price: $11-30
Address: 4A Montpelier Road
Brighton BN1 2LQ, UK
Phone: +44 1273 324065

#364
Shakespeares Head
Cuisines: Pub, British
Average price: $11-30
Address: 1 Chatham Place
Brighton BN1 3TP, UK
Phone: +44 1273 329444

#365
Palm Court
Cuisines: British
Average price: $31-60
Address: Madeira Drive
Brighton BN2 1TW, UK
Phone: +44 872 148 6077

#366
The Empire Tandoori
Cuisines: Fast Food, Indian
Average price: $11-30
Address: 76 Lewes Road
Brighton BN2 3HZ, UK
Phone: +44 1273 687400

#367
Black Lion
Cuisines: Pub, GastroPub, British
Average price: $11-30
Address: 14 Black Lion Street
Brighton BN1 1ND, UK
Phone: +44 1273 711884

#368
The Dugout
Cuisines: Pizza, Sports Bar
Average price: $11-30
Address: 106 Lewes Road
Brighton BN2 3QA, UK
Phone: +44 1273 622310

#369
Eastern Eye
Cuisines: Indian, Ethnic Food
Average price: $11-30
Address: 58 London Road
Brighton BN1 4JE, UK
Phone: +44 1273 685151

#370
Sobs
Cuisines: Fast Food, Turkish
Average price: $11-30
Address: 3 Islingword Road
Brighton BN2 9SE, UK
Phone: +44 1273 700088

#371
Aroma Spice
Cuisines: Indian, Fast Food
Average price: Under $10
Address: 4 Lewes Rd
Brighton BN2 3HP, UK
Phone: +44 1273 677608

#372
The World's End
Cuisines: Pub, Barbeque
Average price: $11-30
Address: 60-61 London Road
Brighton BN1 4JE, UK
Phone: +44 1273 692311

#373
Grints of Brighton
Cuisines: Coffee & Tea, Bakery
Average price: Under $10
Address: 13 Cranbourne Street
Brighton BN1 2RD, UK
Phone: +44 1273 728091

#374
China Garden Restaurant
Cuisines: Dim Sum
Average price: $11-30
Address: 88-91 Preston Street
Brighton BN1 2HG, UK
Phone: +44 1273 325124

#375
Day's Oriental Buffet
Cuisines: Buffet, Asian Fusion
Average price: $11-30
Address: 75 - 79 East St
Brighton BN1 1NF, UK
Phone: +44 1273 748888

#376
Bombay Aloo Mix
Cuisines: Indian, Pakistani
Average price: Under $10
Address: 119 St James's Street
Brighton BN2 1TH, UK
Phone: +44 1273 622133

#377
Terraces
Cuisines: American
Average price: $11-30
Address: Madeira Dr
Brighton BN2 1PS, UK
Phone: +44 1273 545250

#378
The Daily Catch
Cuisines: Fast Food
Average price: $11-30
Address: 102 St James's Street
Brighton BN2 1TP, UK
Phone: +44 1273 571233

#379
Kemp Spices
Cuisines: Indian, Pakistani, Fast Food
Average price: $11-30
Address: 51 St Georges Road
Brighton BN2 1EF, UK
Phone: +44 1273 623331

#380
Carluccio's
Cuisines: Italian, Coffee & Tea
Average price: $11-30
Address: Jubilee Street
Brighton BN1 1GE, UK
Phone: +44 1273 690493

#381
Banjo's Sandwich Shop
Cuisines: Coffee & Tea, Sandwiches, Breakfast & Brunch
Average price: Under $10
Address: 9 Norfolk Sq
Brighton BN1 2PB, UK
Phone: +44 1273 772836

#382
Buon Appetito
Cuisines: Italian
Average price: $11-30
Address: 81 Western Road
Hove BN3 2JQ, UK
Phone: +44 1273 204848

#383
The Giggling Squid
Cuisines: Thai, Tapas, Seafood
Average price: $11-30
Address: 129 Church Road
Hove BN3 2AE, UK
Phone: +44 1273 771991

#384
La Capannina
Cuisines: Italian
Average price: $11-30
Address: 15 Madeira Place
Brighton BN2 1TN, UK
Phone: +44 1273 680839

#385
Raj Pavillion
Cuisines: Indian
Average price: $31-60
Address: 16 Preston Road
Brighton BN1 4QF, UK
Phone: +44 1273 672255

#386
Graze Restaurant
Cuisines: British, Tapas
Average price: $31-60
Address: 42 Western Road
Hove BN3 1JD, UK
Phone: +44 1273 823707

#387
Topolino's Duo
Cuisines: Italian
Average price: $11-30
Address: 67 Church Road
Hove BN3 2BD, UK
Phone: +44 1273 725726

#388
The Meadow
Cuisines: British, Breakfast & Brunch
Average price: $31-60
Address: 64 Western Road
Hove BN3 2JQ, UK
Phone: +44 1273 721182

#389
Volks Bar & Club
Cuisines: Bar, Nightclub, Cafe
Average price: $11-30
Address: 3 Madeira Drive
Brighton BN2 1PS, UK
Phone: +44 1273 682828

#390
Indian Summer
Cuisines: Indian, Pakistani
Average price: $31-60
Address: East Street
Brighton BN1 1HP, UK
Phone: +44 1273 711001

#391
Hove Tandoori
Cuisines: Indian, Pakistani
Average price: $11-30
Address: 175 Church Road
Hove BN3 2AB, UK
Phone: +44 1273 737188

#392
The Connaught
Cuisines: GastroPub, British
Average price: $11-30
Address: 48 Hove Street
Hove BN3 2DH, UK
Phone: +44 1273 206578

#393
Los Amigos
Cuisines: Mexican, Tex-Mex
Average price: $31-60
Address: 60 Church Road
Hove BN3 2FP, UK
Phone: +44 1273 778777

#394
Saffrons
Cuisines: Indian, Fast Food
Average price: $11-30
Address: 2 Coombe Ter
East Sussex BN2 4AD, UK
Phone: +44 1273 681280

#395
Utopia Cafe
Cuisines: Coffee & Tea, Cafe
Average price: $11-30
Address: 49 Gardner St
Brighton BN1 1UN, UK
Phone: +44 1273 818844

#396
Marrocco's
Cuisines: Italian
Average price: $11-30
Address: 8 Kings Esplanade
Hove BN3 2WA, UK
Phone: +44 1273 203764

#397
Hove Park Deli
Cuisines: Delis, Caterers
Average price: $31-60
Address: 73 Old Shoreham Road
Hove BN3 7BE, UK
Phone: +44 1273 777779

#398
Hove Park
Cuisines: Cafe
Average price: Under $10
Address: Parkview Road
Hove BN3 7BF, UK
Phone: +44 1273 293080

#399
Sabai
Cuisines: Thai
Average price: $11-30
Address: 165-169 Princes House
Brighton BN1 1EA, UK
Phone: +44 1273 773030

#400
Dig in the Ribs
Cuisines: Tex-Mex, Mexican
Average price: $11-30
Address: 47 Preston St
Brighton BN1 2HP, UK
Phone: +44 1273 325275

#401
Le Gourmet
Cuisines: Delis, Coffee & Tea
Average price: Above $61
Address: 159 Dyke Road
Hove BN3 1TJ, UK
Phone: +44 1273 778437

#402
The Garden Cafe
Cuisines: Coffee & Tea, British
Average price: Under $10
Address: St Anns Well Gardens
Brighton and Hove BN3 1RP, UK
Phone: +44 1273 735187

#403
La Tasca
Cuisines: Spanish, Basque
Average price: $31-60
Address: 165 North Street
Brighton BN1 1EA, UK
Phone: +44 1273 737342

#404
Grubbs Burgers
Cuisines: Fast Food
Average price: Under $10
Address: 62 Western Rd
Hove BN3 1JD, UK
Phone: +44 1273 736526

#405
Namul
Cuisines: Korean
Average price: Under $10
Address: 49 Gardner Street
The Lanes BN1 1UN, UK
Phone: +44 1273 973878

#406
The Hove Kitchen
Cuisines: Pub, British, European
Average price: $11-30
Address: 102-105 Western Road
Hove BN3 1FA, UK
Phone: +44 1273 725495

#407
The Green Mango
Cuisines: Thai
Average price: $31-60
Address: 8 Church Rd
Hove BN3 2, UK
Phone: +44 1273 327226

#408
Cowley Club
Cuisines: Vegan, Music Venues
Average price: $11-30
Address: 12 London Road
Brighton BN1 4JA, UK
Phone: +44 872 148 6259

#409
Sichuan Chef
Cuisines: Chinese
Average price: $11-30
Address: 18-19 York Place
Brighton BN1 4GU, UK
Phone: +44 1273 698606

#410
Park Crescent
Cuisines: Pub, British
Average price: $11-30
Address: 39 Park Crescent Terrace
Brighton BN2 3HE, UK
Phone: +44 1273 604993

#411
Our Cornish Pasty Shop
Cuisines: Bakery, Desserts, Fast Food
Average price: Under $10
Address: 24 Gardner Street
Brighton BN1 1UP, UK
Phone: +44 1273 688063

#412
Eat
Cuisines: Coffee & Tea, Cafe
Average price: Under $10
Address: Churchill Square
Brighton and Hove BN1 2RG, UK
Phone: +44 1273 732380

#413
Pizza Fritta
Cuisines: Pizza, Italian
Average price: Under $10
Address: Churchill Square
Brighton and Hove BN1, UK
Phone: +44 1273 719526

#414
The Hove Bank
Steak & Ribs Restaurant
Cuisines: British, Steakhouse
Average price: $11-30
Address: 63 -64 Western Road
Hove BN3, UK
Phone: +44 1273 721182

#415
Wetherspoons
Cuisines: Pub, British
Average price: $11-30
Address: 20-22a West Street
Brighton BN1 2RE, UK
Phone: +44 1273 224690

#416
24 St Georges Restaurant
Cuisines: European
Average price: $31-60
Address: 24-25 St Georges Rd
Brighton BN2 1, UK
Phone: +44 1273 626060

#417
The Bell
Cuisines: Pub, British
Average price: $11-30
Address: 15-17 Belfast Street
Hove BN3 3YS, UK
Phone: +44 1273 770773

#418
Donatello Restaurant
Cuisines: Italian, Pizza
Average price: $11-30
Address: 1-3 Brighton Place
Brighton BN1 1HJ, UK
Phone: +44 1273 775477

#419
Orsino Restaurant
Cuisines: Italian, Steakhouse, Seafood
Average price: $11-30
Address: 141 Church Road
Hove BN3 2AE, UK
Phone: +44 1273 770999

#420
Brighton Pagoda
Cuisines: Chinese
Average price: Above $61
Address: West Quay Brighton Marina
Village BN2 5UF, UK
Phone: +44 1273 819053

#421
The Gladstone
Cuisines: Pub, British, Music Venues
Average price: Under $10
Address: 123 Lewes Road
Brighton BN2 3QB, UK
Phone: +44 4412 7362 0888

#422
Bali Brasserie
Cuisines: Restaurant, Bar
Average price: $11-30
Address: Kingsway Court
Hove BN3 2LP, UK
Phone: +44 1273 323810

#423
Galileo Pizzeria
Cuisines: Italian, Pizza
Average price: $11-30
Address: 1 Woodland Parade
Hove BN3 6DR, UK
Phone: +44 1273 330883

#424
Otello Restaurant
Cuisines: Italian
Average price: $11-30
Address: 122 Church Road
Hove BN3 2EA, UK
Phone: +44 1273 227173

#425
Chip Basket
Cuisines: Fish & Chips
Average price: Under $10
Address: 131 Church Road
Hove BN3 2AE, UK
Phone: +44 1273 734753

#426
Piccolo
Cuisines: Italian
Average price: Under $10
Address: 56 Ship Street
Brighton BN1 1AF, UK
Phone: +44 4412 7338 0380

#427
All In Here
Cuisines: Pizza
Average price: Under $10
Address: 57 North St
Brighton and Hove BN1 1RH, UK
Phone: +44 1273 721200

#428
Indiana Restaurant
Cuisines: Indian, Pakistani
Average price: $11-30
Address: 4 Church Road
Hove BN3 2FL, UK
Phone: +44 1273 731354

#429
The Cricketers
Cuisines: Pub, British
Average price: $11-30
Address: 15 Black Lion Street
Brighton BN1 1ND, UK
Phone: +44 1273 329472

#430
Truffles
Cuisines: Bakery, Coffee & Tea, Breakfast & Brunch
Average price: $11-30
Address: 21 George Street
Hove BN3 3YA, UK
Phone: +44 1273 725686

#431
Crêperie Angélie
Cuisines: Creperies
Average price: Under $10
Address: 9 Duke Street
Brighton BN1 1AH, UK
Phone: +44 1273 325433

#432
Montefiore Fisheries
Cuisines: Fish & Chips
Average price: $11-30
Address: 23 Montefiore Road
Hove BN3 1RD, UK
Phone: +44 1273 324496

#433
Kenzi
Cuisines: Irish, Moroccan
Average price: $11-30
Address: 42 Church Road
Hove BN3 2FN, UK
Phone: +44 1273 733228

#434
Nayeb
Cuisines: Persian/Iranian
Average price: Under $10
Address: 1 The Dr
Hove BN3 3JE, UK
Phone: +44 1273 204020

#435
Vineyard Steak House
Cuisines: Greek, Mediterranean
Average price: $31-60
Address: 64 Preston Street
Brighton BN1 2HE, UK
Phone: +44 1273 321681

#436
Indian Kitchen
Cuisines: Fast Food, Indian
Average price: Under $10
Address: 194 Church Road
Hove BN3 2DJ, UK
Phone: +44 1273 202056

#437
Leonardo Ristorante Italiano
Cuisines: Italian
Average price: Under $10
Address: 55 Church Road
Hove BN3 2BD, UK
Phone: +44 1273 328888

#438
Snackerama Sandwich Bar
Cuisines: Sandwiches
Average price: $11-30
Address: 89 Portland Road
Hove BN3 5DP, UK
Phone: +44 1273 733033

#439
Frankie Vaughns
Cuisines: Sandwiches, Coffee & Tea
Average price: $31-60
Address: 180 Edward Street
Brighton BN2 0JB, UK
Phone: +44 1273 818888

#440
The Nevill of Hove
Cuisines: Pub, Italian, Pizza
Average price: $11-30
Address: 214 Nevill Road
Hove BN3 7QQ, UK
Phone: +44 1273 558799

#441
Yummy Cottage
Cuisines: Thai, Fast Food, Chinese
Average price: $11-30
Address: 4 Leybourne Parade
Brighton and Hove BN2 4LW, UK
Phone: +44 1273 818161

#442
Yo Sushi
Cuisines: Sushi Bar
Average price: $11-30
Address: 6 Jubilee St
Brighton BN1 1GE, UK
Phone: +44 1273 689659

#443
Tandoori Bites
Cuisines: Indian, Fast Food
Average price: $11-30
Address: 5 Victoria Terrace
Brighton BN3 2WB, UK
Phone: +44 1273 773090

#444
64 Degrees
Cuisines: Tapas
Average price: $31-60
Address: 53 Meeting House Lane
Brighton BN1 1HB, UK
Phone: +44 1273 770115

#445
Aristocrats
Cuisines: GastroPub
Average price: Under $10
Address: 54 Preston St
Brighton BN1 2HE, UK
Phone: +44 1273 748388

#446
Cafe Giardino
Cuisines: Fast Food, Italian
Average price: $11-30
Address: Churchill Square
Brighton and Hove BN1 2TE, UK
Phone: +44 1273 749724

#447
Picnics
Cuisines: Cafe, Coffee & Tea
Average price: Under $10
Address: Victoria Terrace
Hove BN3 2WB, UK
Phone: +44 1273 747999

#448
Sini
Cuisines: Mediterranean, Turkish
Average price: $11-30
Address: 5 Hove Manor
Hove BN3 2DF, UK
Phone: +44 1273 724311

#449
Spice Nutriment
Cuisines: Indian, Fast Food
Average price: $11-30
Address: 66 Queens Road
Brighton BN1 3XD, UK
Phone: +44 1273 777746

#450
Balti Express
Cuisines: Fast Food
Average price: Under $10
Address: 72 Beaconsfield Road
Brighton BN1 6DD, UK
Phone: +44 1273 562228

#451
KFC
Cuisines: Fast Food
Average price: Under $10
Address: 107 Blatchington Road
Hove BN3 3YG, UK
Phone: +44 1273 204483

#452
Golden Grill
Cuisines: Fast Food
Average price: $11-30
Address: 91 Church Road
Hove BN3 2BA, UK
Phone: +44 1273 207749

#453
Cafe Venus
Cuisines: Coffee & Tea,
Breakfast & Brunch
Average price: Under $10
Address: 132 Western Road
Hove BN3 1DA, UK
Phone: +44 1273 770017

#454
Fortune House
Cuisines: Fast Food, Chinese, Thai
Average price: Under $10
Address: 83 Blatchington Road
Hove BN3 3YG, UK
Phone: +44 1273 775871

#455
Eddys Take Away Food Shop
Cuisines: Fast Food
Average price: Under $10
Address: 101 Sackville Road
Hove BN3 3WF, UK
Phone: +44 1273 777260

#456
Sky High Fish Bar
Cuisines: Fish & Chips
Average price: Under $10
Address: 246 Portland Road
Hove BN3 5QT, UK
Phone: +44 1273 727692

#457
Sa Sa Fish & Chips
Cuisines: Fish & Chips
Average price: Under $10
Address: 20 Coombe Terrace
Brighton BN2 4AD, UK
Phone: +44 1273 570658

#458
Bangkok Express
Cuisines: Fast Food, Thai
Average price: $11-30
Address: 81 London Road
Brighton BN1 4JF, UK
Phone: +44 1273 696816

#459
Café Delice
Cuisines: Breakfast & Brunch,
Cafe, Brasseries
Average price: $11-30
Address: 40 Kensignton Gardens
Brighton BN1 4AL, UK
Phone: +44 1273 622519

#400
Noori's
Cuisines: Indian
Average price: $11-30
Address: 70-71 Ship Street
Brighton BN1 1AE, UK
Phone: +44 1273 747109

#461
Happy Garden
Cuisines: Chinese
Average price: Under $10
Address: 15 Western Road
Brighton BN3 1AE, UK
Phone: +44 1273 738009

#462
Slug & Lettuce
Cuisines: British
Average price: $11-30
Address: 4-5 George St
Hove BN3 3YA, UK
Phone: +44 1273 733359

#463
Smokeys Brighton
Cuisines: Barbeque
Average price: $11-30
Address: 124 Kings Road The City of Brighton and Hove BN1 2FA, UK
Phone: +44 1273 323888

#464
Wai Kika Moo Kau
Cuisines: Vegetarian, Vegan, Cafe
Average price: $11-30
Address: 11a Kensington Gardens Brighton BN1 4AL, UK
Phone: +44 1273 671117

#465
Latin Lounge
Cuisines: Brazilian, Cuban, Breakfast & Brunch
Average price: $11-30
Address: 14 West Street Brighton BN1 2RQ, UK
Phone: +44 1273 958349

#466
Gourmet Pizza Kitchen
Cuisines: Pizza
Average price: $31-60
Address: 40 Western Road Hove BN3 1JD, UK
Phone: +44 1273 726777

#467
Restaurant Forty One
Cuisines: British
Average price: $11-30
Address: 41 Church Road Hove BN3 2BE, UK
Phone: +44 1273 220663

#468
Caffe Bar Italia
Cuisines: Cafe
Average price: $11-30
Address: 24 George Street Hove BN3 3YA, UK
Phone: +44 7801 098608

#469
Mair Kim's Thai Takeaway
Cuisines: Fast Food
Average price: $11-30
Address: 162 Portland Road Hove BN3 5QL, UK
Phone: +44 1273 323707

#470
Scotties Cafe
Cuisines: Food, Cafe
Average price: Above $61
Address: 194 Portland Road Hove BN3 5QN, UK
Phone: +44 1273 277977

#471
Caffe Nero
Cuisines: Coffee & Tea, Sandwiches
Average price: Under $10
Address: 89a Church Road Hove BN3 2GX, UK
Phone: +44 1273 776626

#472
Al Duomo
Cuisines: Italian, Pizza, Coffee & Tea
Average price: $31-60
Address: 7 Pavilion Buildings Brighton BN1 1EE, UK
Phone: +44 1273 326741

#473
Kemp Town Deli
Cuisines: Delis, Coffee & Tea
Average price: $31-60
Address: 108 St Georges Rd Brighton BN2 1EA, UK
Phone: +44 1273 603411

#474
Pizza Express Restaurant
Cuisines: Pizza, Italian
Average price: $11-30
Address: 107 Church Road Hove BN3 2AF, UK
Phone: +44 1273 770093

#475
Memories of India
Cuisines: Indian, Pakistani
Average price: $11-30
Address: 9b Waterfront Brighton BN2 5WA, UK
Phone: +44 1273 600088

#476
Here
Cuisines: American
Average price: $11-30
Address: 81-82 St James's Street Brighton BN2 1, UK
Phone: +44 1273 693216

#477
Frankie & Benny's
Cuisines: Italian
Average price: $11-30
Address: Unit 3 Waterfront
Brighton BN2 5WA, UK
Phone: +44 1273 688450

#478
Bombay Lounge
Cuisines: Indian, Pakistani
Average price: Under $10
Address: 30-31 North Street
Brighton BN1 1EB, UK
Phone: +44 1273 777355

#479
Albert J Ramsbottom
Cuisines: Fish & Chips
Average price: Under $10
Address: 58 Blatchington Road
Hove BN3 3YH, UK
Phone: +44 1273 725551

#480
Sukhothai Palace
Cuisines: Thai
Average price: $11-30
Address: 62 Middle St
Brighton BN1 1AL, UK
Phone: +44 1273 748448

#481
The White Rabbit
Cuisines: Pub, British, GastroPub
Average price: $31-60
Address: 13 Kensington Gardens
Brighton BN1 4AL, UK
Phone: +44 1273 677655

#482
Giraffe
Cuisines: American
Average price: $11-30
Address: Jubilee St
Brighton BN1 1GE, UK
Phone: +44 1273 688885

#483
A'Maze Oriental
Cuisines: Malaysian, Thai, Japanese
Average price: $11-30
Address: 73a Western Road
Brighton BN1 2, UK
Phone: +44 1273 205777

#484
Zafferelli
Cuisines: Italian, Pizza
Average price: Under $10
Address: 31-32 New Road
Brighton BN1 1UG, UK
Phone: +44 1273 206662

#485
Thai Connection Catering
Cuisines: Thai, Fast Food
Average price: $11-30
Address: 14 Blatchington Road
Hove BN3 3YN, UK
Phone: +44 1273 205009

#486
No 3 Chinese Takeout
Cuisines: Fast Food, Chinese
Average price: $11-30
Address: 184 Sackville Road
Hove BN3 7AL, UK
Phone: +44 1273 202850

#487
Figaro's
Cuisines: Breakfast & Brunch, British
Average price: Under $10
Address: 13 George St
Brighton BN2 1RH, UK
Phone: +44 1273 688811

#488
Latino Restaurant
Cuisines: Spanish, Tapas Bar
Average price: $11-30
Address: 36 Church Road
Hove BN3 2FN, UK
Phone: +44 1273 770355

#489
Thai Orchid
Cuisines: Thai
Average price: $11-30
Address: 65 Preston St
Brighton BN1 2HE, UK
Phone: +44 1273 323224

#490
Havana Spoon
Cuisines: European
Average price: $11-30
Address: 70-72 Church Road
Hove BN3 2FP, UK
Phone: +44 1273 651651

#491
Mykonos Greek Taverna
Cuisines: Greek
Average price: $11-30
Address: 31 Preston Street
Brighton BN1 2HP, UK
Phone: +44 1273 329918

#492
Infinity Foods Cafe
Cuisines: Coffee & Tea, Vegetarian, Breakfast & Brunch
Average price: $11-30
Address: 50 Gardner Street
Brighton BN1 1UN, UK
Phone: +44 1273 670743

#493
Tom's
Cuisines: Coffee & Tea, Sandwiches
Average price: $11-30
Address: Western Road
Hove BN3 2JQ, UK
Phone: +44 1273 748155

#494
Ohso Social
Cuisines: British, Coffee & Tea
Average price: $11-30
Address: 250a Kings Rd Arches
Brighton BN1 1NB, UK
Phone: +44 1273 746067

#495
Atlas Lounge
Cuisines: Coffee & Tea, British, Lounge
Average price: $11-30
Address: 111 Western Road
Brighton BN1 2AA, UK
Phone: +44 871 951 1000

#496
Rotunda Cafe
Cuisines: Coffee & Tea, Sandwiches
Average price: $11-30
Address: 10-11 Preston Street
Brighton BN1 6HN, UK
Phone: +44 1273 555460

#497
Ethels Kitchen
Cuisines: Coffee & Tea, Breakfast & Brunch
Average price: $11-30
Address: 59 Blatchington Road
Hove BN3 3YJ, UK
Phone: +44 1273 203204

#498
China Hins
Cuisines: Chinese
Average price: $31-60
Address: 121 Church Rd
Hove BN3 2AF, UK
Phone: +44 1273 329888

#499
Café 3000
Cuisines: Coffee & Tea, Breakfast & Brunch
Average price: Under $10
Address: 69 Church Rd
Hove BN3 2BB, UK
Phone: +44 1273 773877

#500
El Taco
Cuisines: Tex-Mex, Mexican
Average price: Under $10
Address: 100 Western Road
Brighton BN1 2AA, UK
Phone: +44 1273 725861

TOP 450 ATTRACTIONS

Recommended by Locals & Trevelers
(From #1 to #450)

#1
Brighton Pier
Category: Landmark, Local Flavor
Address: Madeira Dr
Brighton BN2 1TW, UK
Phone: +44 1273 609361

#2
Grey Area
Category: Art Gallery
Average price: Modest
Address: 31 Queens Road
Brighton BN1 3XA, UK

#3
Unitarian Church Brighton
Category: Church
Address: New Road
Brighton BN1 1UF, UK
Phone: +44 1273 696022

#4
Brighton Dome
Category: Performing Arts, Music Venues
Average price: Expensive
Address: Church Street
Brighton BN1, UK
Phone: +44 1273 700747

#5
Ink-d
Category: Art Gallery
Average price: Expensive
Address: 96 North Road
Brighton BN1 1YE, UK
Phone: +44 1273 645299

#6
Bom-Bane's
Category: Coffee & Tea, Music Venues, Belgian
Average price: Expensive
Address: 24 George Street
Brighton BN2 1RH, UK
Phone: +44 1273 606400

#7
Jubilee Library
Category: Library
Address: Jubilee Street
Brighton BN1 1GE, UK
Phone: +44 1273 290800

#8
University of Brighton Gallery
Category: Art Gallery
Average price: Inexpensive
Address: Grand Parade
Brighton BN2 0JY, UK
Phone: +44 1273 643012

#9
Komedia Theatre
Category: Performing Arts
Address: 44-47 Gardner Street
Brighton BN1 1UN, UK
Phone: +44 1273 647101

#10
Artrepublic Art Gallery
Category: Art Gallery, Arts & Crafts
Average price: Modest
Address: 13 Bond Street
Brighton BN1 1RD, UK
Phone: +44 1273 724829

#11
Duke of Yorks Picturehouse
Category: Cinema
Address: Preston Circus
Brighton BN1 4NA, UK
Phone: +44 871 902 5728

#12
Theatre Royal
Category: Performing Arts, Historical Building
Address: New Road
Brighton BN1 1SD, UK
Phone: +44 844 871 7650

#13
Phoenix Art Gallery
Category: Art Gallery
Address: 10-14 Waterloo Place
Brighton BN2 9NB, UK
Phone: +44 1273 603700

#14
St Bartholomew's Church
Category: Church
Address: Ann Street
Brighton BN1 4GP, UK
Phone: +44 1273 620491

#15
Concorde 2
Category: Nightclub, Music Venues
Average price: Modest
Address: Madeira Drive
Brighton BN2 1EN, UK
Phone: +44 1273 673311

#16
Bellis
Category: Art Gallery
Average price: Modest
Address: 8-9 King's Rd
Brighton BN1 1NE, UK
Phone: +44 1273 747429

#17
The Devil's Dyke Inn
Category: Landmark, Historical Building
Address: Dyke Road
Brighton BN1 8YJ, UK
Phone: +44 1273 857256

#18
The Royal Pavilion
Category: Museum
Address: 4/5 Pavilion Buildings
Brighton BN1 1EE, UK
Phone: +44 30 0029 0900

#19
Alexander Gallery
Category: Art Gallery, Arts & Crafts
Average price: Modest
Address: 7 East St
Brighton BN1 1HP, UK
Phone: +44 1273 321694

#20
Hotel Pelirocco
Category: Bar, Hotel, Music Venues
Average price: Expensive
Address: 10 Regency Square
Brighton BN1 2FG, UK
Phone: +44 1273 327055

#21
St Peter's Church
Category: Church
Address: York Place
Brighton BN1 4GU, UK
Phone: +44 1273 698182

#22
Art at Five
Category: Art Gallery
Average price: Expensive
Address: 5 Bartholomews
Brighton BN1 1HG, UK
Phone: +44 1273 774222

#23
Hove Town Hall
Category: Historical Building
Address: Norton Road
Brighton BN3 2, UK
Phone: +44 1273 290000

#24
Brighton Festival Fringe
Category: Performing Arts, Comedy Club
Average price: Modest
Address: 12a Pavilion Buildings
Brighton BN1 1EE, UK
Phone: +44 1273 260832

#25
Chameleon Gallery
Category: Art Gallery
Average price: Expensive
Address: 13a Prince Albert St
Brighton BN1 1HE, UK
Phone: +44 1273 324432

#26
Clarkes Stationers
Category: Cards & Stationery, Printing Services, Arts & Entertainment
Average price: Modest
Address: 11 Bond Street
Brighton BN1 1RD, UK
Phone: +44 1273 728811

#27
The Chapel Royal
Category: Church, Music Venues
Address: 164 North St
Brighton BN1 1, UK
Phone: +44 1273 328767

#28
Brighton & Hove Food and Drink Festival
Category: Festival
Address: 28 Foundry Street
Brighton BN1 4AT, UK
Phone: +44 1273 770044

#29
West Blatchington Windmill
Category: Landmark, Historical Building
Address: Holmes Avenue
Brighton BN3 7LE, UK
Phone: +44 30 0029 0900

#30
Brighton Media Centre
Category: Performing Arts, Recording & Rehearsal Studio, Art Gallery
Address: 15-17 Middle Street
Brighton BN1 1AL, UK
Phone: +44 1273 201100

#31
Cry Of The Gulls
Category: Art Gallery
Average price: Modest
Address: 32 Meeting House Lane
Brighton BN1 1HB, UK
Phone: +44 1273 734347

#32
Artrepublic Art Gallery
Category: Art Gallery, Arts & Crafts
Average price: Modest
Address: 13 Bond Street
Brighton BN1 1RD, UK
Phone: +44 1273 724829

#33
Church of St Nicholas
Category: Church
Address: Dyke Road
Brighton BN1 3LH, UK
Phone: +44 1273 321399

#34
Impure Art
Category: Art Gallery
Address: 13 Ship St Gardens
Brighton BN1 1AJ, UK
Phone: +44 1273 732246

#35
Hove Central Library
Category: Library
Address: 182-186 Church Road
Hove BN3 2EG, UK
Phone: +44 1273 290700

#36
Brighton Museum & Art Gallery
Category: Museum, Art Gallery
Average price: Inexpensive
Address: 4-5 Pavilion Buildings
Brighton BN1 1EE, UK
Phone: +44 30 0029 0900

#37
Artist Residence
Category: Art Gallery, Guest House
Average price: Modest
Address: 33 Regency Sq
Brighton BN1 2GG, UK
Phone: +44 1273 324302

#38
Castor + Pollux
Category: Bookstores, Art Gallery
Average price: Expensive
Address: 164-166 Kings Road Arches
Brighton BN1 1NB, UK
Phone: +44 1273 773776

#39
Volks Railway
Category: Local Flavor, Landmark
Address: 285 Madeira Dr
Brighton BN2 1EN, UK
Phone: +44 1273 292718

#40
Calvary Evangelical Church
Category: Church
Address: 72 Viaduct Road
Brighton BN1 4ND, UK
Phone: +44 1273 682112

#41
Sallis Benney Theatre
Category: Performing Arts, Art Gallery
Average price: Modest
Address: 58-67 Grand Parade
Brighton BN2 0JY, UK
Phone: +44 1273 600900

#42
Fitzherberts
Category: Pub, Music Venues
Average price: Modest
Address: 25 New Road
Brighton BN1 1UG, UK
Phone: +44 1273 682401

#43
Bluedog Gallery
Category: Art Gallery
Average price: Expensive
Address: 20 Gardner Street
Brighton BN1 1UP, UK
Phone: +44 1273 622440

#44
The Bandstand
Category: Landmark, Historical Building
Address: Brighton BN1 2PQ, UK

#45
Pavilion Theatre Brighton
Category: Performing Arts, Music Venues
Address: New Road
Brighton BN1 1UG, UK
Phone: +44 1273 709709

#46
Boxbird Gallery
Category: Art Gallery
Average price: Modest
Address: 14 St. John's Rd
Brighton BN3 2FB, UK
Phone: +44 1273 734295

#47
Seafront Image
Category: Cards & Stationery, Art Gallery
Average price: Expensive
Address: 195 Kings Rd Arches
Brighton BN1 1NB, UK
Phone: +44 1273 725777

#48
St John The Baptist Catholic Church
Category: Church
Address: 2 Bristol Road
Brighton BN2 1AP, UK
Phone: +44 1273 681587

#49
Three and Ten
Category: Comedy Club, Music Venues
Average price: Modest
Address: 10 Steine Street
Brighton BN2 1TE, UK
Phone: +44 1273 609777

#50
Casablanca Jazz Club
Category: Jazz & Blues, Nightclub, Bar
Average price: Inexpensive
Address: 3 Middle Street
Brighton BN1 1AL, UK
Phone: +44 1273 321817

#51
Brighton Clock Tower
Category: Landmark, Historical Building
Address: 32 Church Street
Brighton BN1 1RL, UK
Phone: +44 1273 706010

#52
Fabrica
Category: Performing Arts, Art Gallery, Museum
Average price: Inexpensive
Address: Ship Street
Brighton BN1 1AB, UK
Phone: +44 1273 778646

#53
St Lukes Queens Park
Category: Church
Address: Queens Park Terrace
Brighton BN2 9YA, UK
Phone: +44 1273 603946

#54
Brighton Museum & Art Gallery
Category: Museum, Art Gallery
Average price: Inexpensive
Address: 4-5 Pavilion Buildings
Brighton BN1 1EE, UK
Phone: +44 30 0029 0900

#55
Brighton Sailing Club
Category: Social Club
Address: 109 Kings Road Arches
Brighton BN1 2FN, UK
Phone: +44 1273 321802

#56
Phoenix Arts
Category: Art Gallery, Art Schools
Address: 10-13 Waterloo Pl
Brighton BN2 9NB, UK
Phone: +44 1273 603700

#57
Cine-City: Brighton Film Festival
Category: Cinema, Local Flavor
Address: University of Brighton Grande Parade Brighton BN2 0JY, UK
Phone: +44 1273 644721

#58
Regency Square
Category: Landmark, Historical Building
Address: Brighton
Brighton BN1 2FG, UK

#59
Prescription Art
Category: Art Gallery
Average price: Modest
Address: 16 - 30 Hollingdean Road
Brighton BN2 4AA, UK
Phone: +44 7941 385715

#60
Brighton History Centre
Category: Library
Address: Brighton Museum & Art Gallery
Brighton BN1 1EE, UK
Phone: +44 1273 296972

#61
The Druids Arms
Category: Pub, Music Venues
Average price: Inexpensive
Address: 79-81 Ditchling Road
Brighton BN1 4SD, UK
Phone: +44 1273 680596

#62
The Ranelagh
Category: Jazz & Blues, Pub
Average price: Modest
Address: 2-3 The High Street
Brighton BN2 1RP, UK
Phone: +44 1273 681634

#63
Brighton Photo Biennial
Category: Art Gallery, Cinema
Address: University of Brighton
Brighton BN2 9, UK
Phone: +44 1273 643052

#64
Church Of The Good Shepherd
Category: Religious Organizations
Address: 272 Dyke Road
Brighton BN1 5AE, UK
Phone: +44 1273 882987

#65
Castor + Pollux
Category: Bookstores, Art Gallery, Jewelry
Average price: Expensive
Address: 164-166 Kings Road Arches
Brighton BN1 1NB, UK
Phone: +44 1273 773776

#66
Clifton Terrace
Category: Landmark, Historical Building
Address: Clifton Terrace
Brighton BN1 3HA, UK

#67
Fabrica
Category: Performing Arts, Art Gallery, Museum
Average price: Inexpensive
Address: Ship Street
Brighton BN1 1AB, UK
Phone: +44 1273 778646

#68
Brighton Buddhist Centre
Category: Buddhist Temple, Yoga
Address: 17 Tichborne Street
Brighton BN1 1UR, UK
Phone: +44 1273 772090

#69
Cowley Club
Category: Health Markets, Music Venues, Vegan
Average price: Modest
Address: 12 London Road
Brighton BN1 4JA, UK
Phone: +44 872 148 6259

#70
Brighton Fishing Museum
Category: Museum, Art Gallery
Average price: Modest
Address: 201 Kings Road Arches
Brighton BN1 1NB, UK
Phone: +44 1273 723064

#71
io Gallery
Category: Art Gallery, Arts & Crafts, Flowers & Gifts
Average price: Modest
Address: 39 Sydney Street
Brighton BN1 4EP, UK
Phone: +44 1273 671212

#72
Patcham Clock Tower
Category: Landmark, Historical Building
Address: Ladies Mile Rd
Brighton BN1 8, UK

#73
Brighton Toy & Model Museum
Category: Museum
Address: 52-55 Trafalgar Street
Brighton BN1 4EB, UK
Phone: +44 1273 749494

#74
Crane Kalman Brighton
Category: Art Gallery
Average price: Expensive
Address: 38 Kensington Gardens
Brighton BN1 4AL, UK
Phone: +44 1273 697096

#75
St Nicolas & St Andrew Church
Category: Church
Address: South Street
Brighton BN41 2LE, UK
Phone: +44 1273 418090

#76
The Hope
Category: Music Venues, Lounge, Pub
Average price: Inexpensive
Address: 10-12 Queens Road
Brighton BN1 3WA, UK
Phone: +44 872 148 5838

#77
Hush Art Cafe
Category: Art Gallery
Address: Castle St
Brighton BN1 2HW, UK
Phone: +44 1273 772427

#78
Odeon Cinemas
Category: Cinema
Address: West Road
Brighton BN1 2RE, UK
Phone: +44 871 224 4007

#79
Foredown Tower
Category: Landmark, Historical Building
Address: Foredown Road
Brighton BN41 2EW, UK
Phone: +44 1273 415625

#80
Ambience Gallery
Category: Art Gallery
Address: 38 Meeting House Ln
Brighton BN1 1HB, UK
Phone: +44 1273 776607

#81
St Johns Church
Category: Church
Address: Knoyle Road
Brighton BN1 6RB, UK
Phone: +44 1273 553311

#82
Latest Music Bar
Category: Music Venues
Average price: Modest
Address: 14 - 17 Manchester Street
Brighton BN2 1TF, UK
Phone: +44 1273 687171

#83
Blue Dog Gallery
Category: Art Gallery
Address: 20 Gardner Street
Brighton BN1 1UP, UK
Phone: +44 1273 622440

#84
The Marlborough
Category: Gay Bar, Cinema
Address: 4 Princes Street
Brighton BN2 1RD, UK
Phone: +44 1273 570028

#85
Kiss Wall
Category: Landmark
Address: Seafront
Brighton BN1 1, UK

#86
Jeremy Sanders
Category: Art Gallery
Address: 237 Kings Road Arches
Brighton BN1 1NB, UK
Phone: +44 1273 777340

#87
Brighton Central Library
Category: Library
Address: New England St
Brighton BN1 4GH, UK
Phone: +44 1273 290800

#88

Theatre Royal
Category: Performing Arts, Landmark, Historical Building
Address: New Road
Brighton BN1 1SD, UK
Phone: +44 844 871 7650

#89

Two Kats & A Cow
Category: Art Gallery
Average price: Expensive
Address: 167 Kings Rd Arches
Brighton BN1 1NB, UK
Phone: +44 1273 776746

#90

Oasis Christian Fellowship
Category: Church
Address: Hangleton Way
Brighton BN3 8AG, UK
Phone: +44 1273 411116

#91

The Hobgoblin
Category: Pub, Music Venues
Average price: Inexpensive
Address: 31 York Place
Brighton BN1 4GU, UK
Phone: +44 1273 682933

#92

St. Pauls Church
Category: Church
Address: 9 Russell Place
Brighton BN1 2RG, UK
Phone: +44 1273 739639

#93

Brighton Framing Gallery
Category: Framing, Art Gallery
Average price: Modest
Address: 103 St Georges Rd
Brighton BN2 1EA, UK
Phone: +44 1273 696221

#94

Brighton Festival
Category: Performing Arts, Jazz & Blues, Festival
Address: 29 New Road
Brighton BN1 1UG, UK
Phone: +44 1273 700747

#95

Zorian Gallery
Category: Art Gallery
Address: 246 Kings Rd Arches
Brighton BN1 1NB, UK
Phone: +44 1273 710881

#96

Dorset Gardens Methodist Church
Category: Church
Address: Dorset Gardens
Brighton BN2 1RL, UK
Phone: +44 1273 605502

#97

Corn Exchange
Category: Performing Arts, Music Venues
Average price: Modest
Address: Church Street
Brighton BN1 1UE, UK
Phone: +44 1273 700747

#98

Open Art Gallery Cafe
Category: Art Gallery, Cafe
Address: 6 Nevill Road
Brighton BN2 7HG, UK
Phone: +44 1273 965364

#99

Appendage Fashion Shops
Category: Fashion, Art Gallery
Average price: Modest
Address: 36 Kensington Gardens
Brighton BN1 4AL, UK
Phone: +44 1273 605901

#100

Sussex Square and Lewes Crescent
Category: Landmark, Historical Building
Address: Sussex Square Lewes Crescent
Brighton BN2 5AA, UK

#101

Royal Pavilion Tavern
Category: Nightclub, Music Venues
Average price: Inexpensive
Address: 7-8 Castle Square
Brighton BN1 1FX, UK
Phone: +44 1273 827641

#102
Daniel Laurence Home & Garden
Category: Art Gallery, Home Decor
Average price: Expensive
Address: 226 Kings Rd Arches
Brighton BN1 1NB, UK
Phone: +44 1273 739694

#103
Fairtrade Gallery
Category: Art Gallery, Framing
Average price: Modest
Address: 26 Montague Pl
Brighton BN2 1JE, UK
Phone: +44 7990 511576

#104
York Place Studio
Category: Art Gallery
Address: 28 York Pl
Brighton BN1 4GU, UK
Phone: +44 1273 674758

#105
Gallery 94
Category: Art Gallery
Address: 94 North Rd
Brighton BN41 2, UK
Phone: +44 1273 675991

#106
Digital
Category: Nightclub, Music Venues
Average price: Expensive
Address: 187-193 Kings Rd Arches
Brighton BN1 1NB, UK
Phone: +44 1273 227763

#107
St. Peter's House Library
Category: Library
Address: 16-18 Richmond Place
Brighton BN2 9NA, UK
Phone: +44 1273 643221

#108
St Georges Church
Category: Church
Address: St Georges Rd
Brighton BN2 1ED, UK
Phone: +44 1273 279448

#109
Proud Cabaret Brighton
Category: Nightclub, Music Venues
Average price: Modest
Address: 83 St Georges Road
Brighton BN2 1EF, UK
Phone: +44 1273 605789

#110
George Street Gallery
Category: Framing, Art Gallery
Address: 4 George Street
Brighton BN2 1RH, UK
Phone: +44 1273 681852

#111
Pretty Eccentric
Category: Art Gallery, Furniture Stores
Average price: Expensive
Address: 26 N Street
Brighton BN1 1EB, UK
Phone: +44 7870 607925

#112
Passacaglia
Category: Landmark
Address: Middle Street
Brighton BN1 1, UK

#113
Prince Albert
Category: Pub, Nightclub,
Music Venues
Average price: Modest
Address: 48 Trafalgar Street
Brighton BN1 4ED, UK
Phone: +44 1273 730499

#114
Pretty Eccentric
Category: Art Gallery, Furniture Stores
Average price: Expensive
Address: 26 N Street
Brighton BN1 1EB, UK
Phone: +44 7870 607925

#115
Stanmer Church
Category: Church
Address: Stanmer Village
Brighton BN1 9PZ, UK
Phone: +44 1273 606928

#116
Expo
Category: Home Decor, Cards & Stationery, Art Gallery
Average price: Modest
Address: Churchill Sq
Brighton BN1 2TF, UK
Phone: +44 1273 726347

#117
University Of Brighton Gallery
Category: Art Gallery
Average price: Inexpensive
Address: Grand Parade
Brighton BN2 0JY, UK
Phone: +44 1273 643012

#118
Regency Square
Category: Landmark, Historical Building
Address: Regency Ssqare
Brighton BN1 2, UK

#120
St Joseph's Catholic Church
Category: Church
Address: Elm Grove
Brighton BN2 3AA, UK
Phone: +44 1273 386159

#121
Brighton Fishing Quarter Gallery
Category: Local Flavor, Art Gallery
Average price: Modest
Address: Brighton Fishing Quarter
Brighton BN1 1NB, UK

#122
JAG Studio & Gallery
Category: Art Gallery
Average price: Modest
Address: 283A Madeira Dr
Brighton BN2 1PT, UK
Phone: +44 7810 523984

#123
Ink-d
Category: Art Gallery
Average price: Expensive
Address: 96 North Road
Brighton BN1 1YE, UK
Phone: +44 1273 645299

#124
St Wulfran's C of E Church
Category: Church, Historical Building
Address: The Green off Greenways
Brighton BN2 7BA, UK

#125
Banksy Graffiti
Category: Art Gallery
Address: 48 Trafalgar St
Brighton BN1 1RD, UK

#126
Phoenix Arts
Category: Art Gallery, Art Schools
Address: 10-13 Waterloo Pl
Brighton BN2 9NB, UK
Phone: +44 1273 603700

#127
Preston Manor
Category: Museum
Address: Preston Road
Brighton BN1 6SD, UK

#128
Witch Ball
Category: Antiques, Home Decor, Art Gallery
Average price: Modest
Address: 48 Meeting House Lane
Brighton BN1 1HB, UK
Phone: +44 1273 326618

#129
The Brighton Coalition
Category: Nightclub, Music Venues
Average price: Modest
Address: 171-181 Kings Rd Arches
Brighton BN1 1NB, UK
Phone: +44 1273 772842

#130
The Brunswick Estate
Category: Hotel, Historical Building
Address: Brunswick Square
Hove BN3 1EH, UK
Phone: +44 1273 763838

#131
St Phillp C of E Church
Category: Church
Address: New Church Road
Hove BN3 4BB, UK
Phone: +44 1273 737915

#132
Artists Open House
Category: Local Flavor, Art Gallery
Average price: Modest
Address: Artists Open House.
Brighton BN50 9DF, UK

#133
Festival Children's Parade
Category: Performing Arts, Local Flavor
Address: Brighton
Brighton BN1 1UG, UK
Phone: +44 1273 709709

#134
Cub Culture
Category: Art Gallery
Address: 28 York Place Studio
Brighton BN1 4GU, UK

#135
Acaster Langridge
Category: Art Gallery
Address: 243 Kings Rd Arches
Brighton BN1 1NB, UK

#136
Adelaide Mansions
Category: Historical Building
Address: Adelaide Mansions
Hove BN3 2GT, UK

#137
The World's End
Category: Pub, Music Venues
Average price: Modest
Address: 60-61 London Road
Brighton BN1 4JE, UK
Phone: +44 1273 692311

#138
First Light
Category: Art Gallery
Address: 3 Nile Street
Brighton BN1 1HW, UK
Phone: +44 1273 327344

#139
St Andrews Old Church Hove
Category: Church
Address: Church Road
Hove BN3 3YT, UK
Phone: +44 1273 734859

#140
The Warren
Category: Music Venues
Average price: Modest
Address: 48-50 Russell Place
Brighton BN1 2RG, UK
Phone: +44 7800 983290

#141
The Art Space
Category: Art Gallery
Address: 94-101 London Road
Brighton BN1 4LB, UK
Phone: +44 1273 623413

#142
St Andrew's Chapel
Category: Church
Address: Waterloo Street
Hove BN3 1AQ, UK

#143
Brighton Media Centre
Category: Performing Arts, Recording & Rehearsal Studio, Art Gallery
Address: 15-17 Middle Street
Brighton BN1 1AL, UK
Phone: +44 1273 201100

#144
Naked Eye
Category: Art Gallery
Average price: Modest
Address: 5 Farm Mews
Hove BN3 1GH, UK
Phone: +44 1273 204800

#145
io Gallery
Category: Art Gallery, Arts & Crafts, Flowers & Gifts
Average price: Modest
Address: 39 Sydney Street
Brighton BN1 4EP, UK
Phone: +44 1273 671212

#146
Stanmer Park
Category: Parks
Address: A270 Lewes Road
Brighton BN1 9SE, UK

#147
Phoenix Art Gallery
Category: Art Gallery
Address: 10-14 Waterloo Place
Brighton BN2 9NB, UK
Phone: +44 1273 603700

#148
Peace Statue
Category: Landmark
Address: Kings Rd
Brighton BN1, UK

#149
Christmas Artists Open House
Category: Local Flavor, Art Gallery
Average price: Modest
Address: PO Box 2781
Brighton BN50 9DF, UK

#150
Brighton Arts Club
Category: Art Gallery, Social Club, Party & Event Planning
Average price: Modest
Address: 43 Providence Place
Brighton BN1 4GE, UK
Phone: +44 7757 781957

#151
Preston Manor
Category: Church
Address: Preston Drove
Brighton BN1 6SD, UK
Phone: +44 30 0029 0900

#152
Brighton Little Theatre
Category: Performing Arts, Music Venues
Average price: Inexpensive
Address: 9 Clarence Gardens
Brighton BN1 2EG, UK
Phone: +44 1273 777748

#153
The Old Picture Shop
Category: Art Gallery
Address: 2 Nile Street
Brighton BN1 1HW, UK
Phone: +44 1273 726600

#154
Church of St Michael and All Angels, Southwick
Category: Church
Address: Church Lane
Shoreham-by-Sea BN42 4GD, UK
Phone: +44 1273 597699

#155
Booth Museum of Natural History
Category: Museum, Art Gallery
Average price: Inexpensive
Address: 194 Dyke Road
Brighton BN1 5AA, UK
Phone: +44 30 0029 0200

#156
Fish Tail Neon
Category: Electronics, Art Gallery
Address: 282 Madeira Drive Arches
Brighton BN2 1DZ, UK
Phone: +44 1273 694662

#157
Brighton Fishing Museum
Category: Museum, Art Gallery
Average price: Modest
Address: 201 Kings Road Arches
Brighton BN1 1NB, UK
Phone: +44 1273 723064

#158
Palmeira Square
Category: Parks
Address: Palmeira Square
Brighton BN3 2, UK

#159
Big Art
Category: Art Gallery
Address: 73 Trafalgar Street
Brighton BN1 4EB, UK
Phone: +44 1273 606044

#160
St Peter's C of E Church
Category: Church
Address: Hangleton Road
Hove BN3 7LQ, UK
Phone: +44 1273 732459

#161
Western Front
Category: Pub, Social Club, British
Average price: Inexpensive
Address: 11 Cranbourne St
Brighton BN1 2RD, UK
Phone: +44 1273 725656

#162
St Julian's Church
Category: Church
Address: Rectory Road
Shoreham-by-Sea BN43 6EB, UK
Phone: +44 1273 593167

#163
Booth Museum Of Natural History
Category: Museum, Art Gallery
Average price: Inexpensive
Address: 194 Dyke Road
Brighton BN1 5AA, UK
Phone: +44 30 0029 0200

#164
More
Category: Music Venues, Wine Bar
Average price: Modest
Address: 98 Trafalgar Street
Brighton BN1 4ER, UK
Phone: +44 1273 693377

#165
Bellis
Category: Art Gallery
Average price: Modest
Address: 8-9 King's Rd
Brighton BN1 1NE, UK
Phone: +44 1273 747429

#166
No Walls Gallery
Category: Art Gallery
Address: 114 Church Street
Brighton BN1 1UD, UK
Phone: +44 1273 324432

#167
Hove Museum & Art Gallery
Category: Museum
Address: 194 Church Road
Brighton BN1 1BA, UK
Phone: +44 1273 290200

#168
Daniel Laurence Home & Garden
Category: Art Gallery, Home Decor
Average price: Expensive
Address: 226 Kings Rd Arches
Brighton BN1 1NB, UK
Phone: +44 1273 739694

#169
North Star Studio Printmaking Co-Operative
Category: Art Gallery
Average price: Inexpensive
Address: 65 Ditchling Rd
Brighton BN1 4SD, UK
Phone: +44 1273 601041

#170
Blue Dog Gallery
Category: Art Gallery
Address: 20 Gardner Street
Brighton BN1 1UP, UK
Phone: +44 1273 622440

#171
Frame of Mind
Category: Framing, Art Gallery
Average price: Modest
Address: 2A Blatchington Rd
Brighton BN3 3YN, UK
Phone: +44 1273 776329

#172
Crane Kalman Brighton
Category: Art Gallery
Average price: Expensive
Address: 38 Kensington Gardens
Brighton BN1 4AL, UK
Phone: +44 1273 697096

#173
Eclectia
Category: Art Gallery
Address: 3 Mermaid Walk
Brighton BN2 5WA, UK
Phone: +44 7734 593393

#174
Bigart
Category: Art Gallery
Address: 73 Trafalgar Street
Brighton BN1 4EB, UK
Phone: +44 1273 606044

#175
Alexander Gallery
Category: Art Gallery,
Arts & Crafts, Home Decor
Average price: Modest
Address: 7 East St
Brighton BN1 1HP, UK
Phone: +44 1273 321694

#176
Framework
Category: Art Gallery
Average price: Modest
Address: 26 Kensington Gardens
Brighton BN1 4AL, UK
Phone: +44 1273 818585

#177
New Venture Theatre
Category: Performing Arts
Address: Bedford Place
Brighton BN1 2PT, UK
Phone: +44 1273 746118

#178
Funky Buddha Lounge
Category: Art Gallery, Nightclub
Average price: Modest
Address: Kings Road Arches
Brighton BN1 1FL, UK

#179
Caia Matheson Artist
Category: Art Gallery
Average price: Modest
Address: Beaconsfield Studio
Brighton BN1 4QL, UK
Phone: +44 7961 405351

#180
The Hydrant
Category: Pub, Nightclub
Average price: Inexpensive
Address: 75 London Road
Brighton BN1 4JF, UK
Phone: +44 1273 608313

#181
Add the Colour
Category: Coffee & Tea, Art Gallery
Average price: Inexpensive
Address: 64-65 North Road
Brighton BN1 1YD, UK
Phone: +44 7817 850202

#182
The Engine Room
Category: Music Venues, Nightclub
Average price: Modest
Address: 5 Preston St
Brighton BN1 2HX, UK
Phone: +44 1273 728999

#183
Edited
Category: Home Decor,
Furniture Stores, Art Gallery
Address: 3 Gardner Street
Brighton BN1 1UP, UK
Phone: +44 1273 604006

#184
St Georges Church
Category: Local Flavor, Music Venues
Average price: Modest
Address: St Georges Rd
Brighton BN2 1ED, UK
Phone: +44 1273 279448

#185
Richard Whadcock
Category: Art Gallery, Cultural Center
Address: 10-14 Waterloo Place
Brighton BN2 9NB, UK
Phone: +44 7726 342610

#186
The Basement
Category: Venues & Event Spaces,
Performing Arts
Address: 24 Kensington Street
Brighton BN1 4AJ, UK
Phone: +44 1273 699733

#187
Art at Five
Category: Art Gallery
Average price: Expensive
Address: 5 Bartholomews
Brighton BN1 1HG, UK
Phone: +44 1273 774222

#188
Cloud Gallery
Category: Art Gallery
Address: 18
Brighton Place
Brighton BN1 1HJ, UK
Phone: +44 7917 886477

#189
Jilted Dog Gallery
Category: Art Gallery
Address: 46 New England Road
Brighton BN1 4GG, UK
Phone: +44 4479 4644 4296

#190
Appendage Fashion Shops
Category: Fashion, Art Gallery, Home Decor
Average price: Modest
Address: 36 Kensington Gardens
Brighton BN1 4AL, UK
Phone: +44 1273 605901

#191
Taylor Made Frames
Category: Art Gallery
Address: 3 Brighton Square
Brighton and Hove BN3 1HD, UK
Phone: +44 1273 739409

#192
Artist Residence
Category: Art Gallery, Guest House
Average price: Modest
Address: 33 Regency Sq
Brighton BN1 2GG, UK
Phone: +44 1273 324302

#193
Suzart
Category: Art Gallery
Address: 280 Suzart at the Jag Gallery
Brighton BN2, UK
Phone: +44 7530 672888

#194
Coach House in Kemptown
Category: Art Gallery
Address: 22 Walpole Road
Brighton BN2 0EA, UK

#195
The Chapel Royal
Category: Music Venues, Churches
Address: 164 North St
Brighton BN1 1, UK
Phone: +44 1273 328767

#196
Fishtail Neon
Category: Art Gallery
Address: 282 Madeira Drive Arches
Brighton BN2 1EN, UK

#197
Sallis Benney Theatre
Category: Performing Arts, Art Gallery
Average price: Modest
Address: 58-67 Grand Parade
Brighton BN2 0JY, UK
Phone: +44 1273 600900

#198
Cry of The Gulls
Category: Art Gallery
Average price: Modest
Address: 32 Meeting House Lane
Brighton BN1 1HB, UK
Phone: +44 1273 734347

#200
Gallery 73
Category: Art Gallery, Arts & Crafts
Address: 73 St James St
Brighton BN2 1PJ, UK

#201
Cineworld
Category: Cinema
Address:
Brighton Marina
Brighton BN2 5UF, UK
Phone: +44 1273 818094

#202
Two Kats & A Cow
Category: Art Gallery
Average price: Expensive
Address: 167 Kings Rd Arches
Brighton BN1 1NB, UK
Phone: +44 1273 776746

#203
Rarekind Art Gallery
Category: Art Gallery, Pub
Address: 102 North Road
Brighton BN1 1YE, UK
Phone: +44 1273 818170

#204
Brighton Artists Gallery
Category: Art Gallery, Bar
Address: 108a Dyke Road
Brighton BN1 3TE, UK
Phone: +44 1273 711016

#205
Seafront Image
Category: Cards & Stationery, Art Gallery
Average price: Expensive
Address: 195 Kings Rd Arches
Brighton BN1 1NB, UK
Phone: +44 1273 725777

#206
Boxbird Gallery
Category: Art Gallery
Average price: Modest
Address: 14 St. John's Rd
Brighton BN3 2FB, UK
Phone: +44 1273 734295

#207
Start Gallery
Category: Art Gallery
Address: 8 Church Street
Brighton BN1 1US, UK
Phone: +44 1273 233984

#208
Art Pool Gallery
Category: Art Gallery
Address: 2 Pool Valley
Brighton BN1 1NJ, UK
Phone: +44 1273 777887

#209
Lighthouse Arts & Training
Category: Performing Arts
Address: 28 Kensington St
Brighton BN1 4AJ, UK
Phone: +44 1273 686320

#210
Clairmonte Gallery
Category: Art Gallery
Address: 56 Gardner St
Brighton BN1 1UN, UK
Phone: +44 1273 622027

#211
Brighton Ballroom
Category: British, Music Venues
Address: 83 St Georges Rd
Brighton BN2 1EF, UK
Phone: +44 1273 605789

#212
The ONCA Gallery
Category: Art Gallery
Address: 14 St George's Place
Brighton BN1 4GB, UK
Phone: +44 1273 958291

#213
Impure Art
Category: Art Gallery
Address: 13 Ship St Gardens
Brighton BN1 1AJ, UK
Phone: +44 1273 732246

#214
Window Gallery
Category: Art Gallery
Address: Dyke Road
Brighton BN1 3JD, UK
Phone: +44 1273 726190

#215
Irish Folk Night
Category: Music Venues, Local Flavor
Address: 13-14 Foundry St
Brighton BN1 4AT, UK
Phone: +44 1273 697014

#216
Quod Art
Category: Art Gallery
Address: 160 North Street
Brighton BN1 1EZ, UK
Phone: +44 1273 772002

#217
Hove Museum & Art Gallery
Category: Museum
Address: 194 Church Road
Brighton BN1 1BA, UK
Phone: +44 1273 290200

#218
Best of Sussex
Category: Art Gallery
Address: 30 New Road
Brighton BN1 1BN, UK

#219
National Association of Railway Club
Category: Social Club
Address: 4 Belmont Dyke Road
Brighton BN1 3TF, UK
Phone: +44 1273 328682

#220
O Contemporary
Category: Art Gallery
Address: 80 Trafalgar Street
Brighton BN1 4EB, UK
Phone: +44 1273 698500

#221
Frame of Mind
Category: Framing, Art Gallery
Average price: Modest
Address: 2A Blatchington Rd
Brighton BN3 3YN, UK
Phone: +44 1273 776329

#222
The Artist Quarter
Category: Art Gallery
Address: Kings Road Arches
Brighton BN1 1NS, UK

#223
Brighton Arts Club
Category: Art Gallery, Social Club, Party & Event Planning
Average price: Modest
Address: 43 Providence Place
Brighton BN1 4GE, UK
Phone: +44 7757 781957

#224
Surrounds
Category: Art Gallery
Address: 8 Little East Street
Brighton BN1 1HT, UK
Phone: +44 1273 327843

#225
The Old Picture Shop
Category: Art Gallery
Address: 2 Nile Street
Brighton BN1 1HW, UK
Phone: +44 1273 725609

#227
Artist Quarter Under the Arches
Category: Irish, Art Gallery
Address: 280 - Brighton BN2 1WP, UK

#228
Fitzherbert Of Brighton
Category: Florists, Art Gallery
Address: 15 Beacon Hill
Brighton BN2 7BN, UK
Phone: +44 1273 302233

#229
The Old Police Cells Museum
Category: Museum
Address: Bartholomew Square
Brighton BN1 1JA, UK
Phone: +44 1273 291052

#230
N Emery
Category: Art Gallery
Address: 231 Kings Road Arches
Brighton BN1 1NB, UK
Phone: +44 1273 735927

#231
Gilburt
Category: Art Gallery
Address: Madeira Drive
Brighton BN2 1PS, UK
Phone: +44 1273 621777

#232
Brighton Fishing Quarter Gallery
Category: Performing Arts
Address: 205 King Road Arches
Brighton BN1 1NB, UK
Phone: +44 1273 730182

#233
Muse Fine Art & Design
Category: Art Gallery
Address: 12 Newmarket Road
Brighton BN2 3QF, UK
Phone: +44 1273 671450

#234
Chameleon Gallery
Category: Art Gallery
Average price: Expensive
Address: 13a Prince Albert St
Brighton BN1 1HE, UK
Phone: +44 1273 324432

#235
Pop! Portraits
Category: Art Gallery
Address: 74 Bramble Rise
Brighton BN1 5GF, UK
Phone: +44 7791 104215

#236
Ikon Gallery
Category: Art Gallery
Address: 3 Albany Mews
Brighton BN3 2PQ, UK
Phone: +44 1273 775630

#237
Born Bad
Category: Music Venues, Local Flavor
Address: Komedia, 44-47 Gardner St
Brighton BN1 1UN, UK
Phone: +44 1273 647100

#238
Art Asylum
Category: Art Gallery
Address: 14a Chesham Road
Brighton BN2 1NB, UK
Phone: +44 1273 626426

#239
Ghost Walk of the Lanes
Category: Performing Arts
Address: 9 Brighton Place
Brighton BN1 1HJ, UK
Phone: +44 1273 328297

#240
Witch Ball
Category: Antiques, Home Decor, Art Gallery
Average price: Modest
Address: 48 Meeting House Lane
Brighton BN1 1HB, UK
Phone: +44 1273 326618

#241
Jennie Ricketts
Category: Art Gallery
Address: Arundel Place
Brighton BN2 1GG, UK
Phone: +44 1273 605070

#242
The Grange
Category: Art Gallery
Address: The Green
Brighton BN2 7HA, UK
Phone: +44 1273 301004

#244
One Eyed Jacks
Category: Art Gallery
Address: 28 York Place
North Laine BN1 4GU, UK
Phone: +44 7743 098530

#245
Brighton Photo Biennial
Category: Local Flavor, Art Gallery, Cinema
Address: University of Brighton
Brighton BN2 9, UK
Phone: +44 1273 643052

#246
Palmeira Gallery
Category: Art Gallery
Address: 71a Western Road
Hove BN3 2JQ, UK
Phone: +44 1273 325143

#247
Brighton Music Hall
Category: Bar, Music Venues
Average price: Inexpensive
Address: 127 Kings Road Arches
Brighton BN1 2FN, UK
Phone: +44 1273 747287

#248
Arthouse Gallery
Category: Art Gallery
Address: 10 Western Road
Hove BN3 1AE, UK
Phone: +44 1273 770083

#249
Penny Arcade Museum
Category: Local Flavor, Museum
Address: Kings Rd Arches
Brighton BN1, UK
Phone: +44 1273 608620

#250
Artizan Editions
Category: Art Gallery
Address: Conway St
Hove BN3 3LW, UK
Phone: +44 1273 773959

#251
Brighton Framing Gallery
Category: Framing, Art Gallery
Average price: Modest
Address: 103 St Georges Rd
Brighton BN2 1EA, UK
Phone: +44 1273 696221

#252
Fairtrade Gallery
Category: Art Gallery, Framing
Average price: Modest
Address: 26 Montague Pl
Brighton BN2 1JE, UK
Phone: +44 7990 511576

#253
Preston Brewery Tap
Category: Pub, Sports Bar, Music Venues
Address: 197 Preston Road
Brighton BN1 6SA, UK
Phone: +44 1273 508700

#254
Prescription Art
Category: Art Gallery
Average price: Modest
Address: 16 - 30 Hollingdean Road
Brighton BN2 4AA, UK
Phone: +44 7941 385715

#255
Ace Cafe Brighton Burn Up
Category: Automotive
Address: Madeira Drive
Brighton BN2 1, UK

#256
Brighton Centre
Category: Music Venues, Performing Arts
Average price: Modest
Address: Kings Rd
Brighton BN1 2GR, UK
Phone: +44 1273 290131

#258
Quaff Fine Wine Merchant
Category: Shopping, Wineries
Address: 139/141 Portland Road
Brighton BN3 5QJ, UK
Phone: +44 1273 820320

#259
Green Door Store
Category: Music Venues
Address: Units 2 3 4 Trafalgar Arches
Brighton BN1 3XP, UK
Phone: +44 7944 693214

#260
The Penthouse
Category: Nightclub, Music Venues, Lounge
Average price: Modest
Address: 1 Phoenix Pl
Brighton BN2 9ND, UK
Phone: +44 872 148 6028

#261
Xuma
Category: Music Venues
Average price: Modest
Address: 108a Dyke Road
Brighton BN1 3TE, UK
Phone: +44 4412 7372 4036

#262
Expo
Category: Home Decor, Cards & Stationery, Art Gallery
Average price: Modest
Address: Churchill Sq
Brighton BN1 2TF, UK
Phone: +44 1273 726347

#263
The Rendezvous Casino
Category: Casino
Address: Brighton Marina Village
Brighton BN2 5UT, UK
Phone: +44 1273 605602

#265
Bluedog Gallery
Category: Art Gallery
Average price: Expensive
Address: 20 Gardner Street
Brighton BN1 1UP, UK
Phone: +44 1273 622440

#266
3D-Roadshow
Category: Music & DVDs
Address: 45 Norwich Drive
Brighton BN2 4LB, UK
Phone: +44 1273 681722

#267
Emporium
Category: Performing Arts, Cafe
Average price: Modest
Address: 88 London Road
Brighton BN1 4, UK

#268
Zorian Gallery
Category: Art Gallery
Address: 246 Kings Rd Arches
Brighton BN1 1NB, UK
Phone: +44 1273 710881

#269
Chequers
Category: Pub, Music Venues
Address: 45 Preston Street
Brighton BN1 2HP, UK
Phone: +44 1273 220855

#270
The Hydrant
Category: Sports Bar, Music Venues
Average price: Modest
Address: 75 London Road
Brighton BN1 4JF, UK
Phone: +44 1273 608313

#271
Grosvenor Casino
Category: Casino, Nightlife
Address: 9 Grand Junction Road
Brighton BN1 1PP, UK
Phone: +44 1273 326514

#272
Lambic Arts Theatre
Category: Performing Arts
Address: 36 Gardner Street
Brighton BN1 1UN, UK
Phone: +44 1273 572101

#273
Brighton Festival of World Sacred Music
Category: Festival
Address: 6 Gloucester Street
Brighton BN1 4EW, UK
Phone: +44 1273 252725

#274
York Place Studio
Category: Art Gallery
Address: 28 York Pl
Brighton BN1 4GU, UK
Phone: +44 1273 674758

#275
John Peel Mural
Category: Local Flavor
Address: Frederick Pl
Brighton BN1 1RD, UK

#276
The Art Space
Category: Art Gallery
Address: 94-101 London Road
Brighton BN1 4LB, UK
Phone: +44 1273 623413

#277
Brighton Rock
Category: Performing Arts
Address: 41 Kings Road
Brighton BN1 1NA, UK
Phone: +44 1273 732224

#278
Loop
Category: Music Venues
Address: 12A Pavilion Buildings
Brighton BN1 1EE, UK
Phone: +44 1273 700747

#279
North Star Studio Printmaking Co-Operative
Category: Gallery
Average price: Inexpensive
Address: 65 Ditchling Rd
Brighton BN1 4SD, UK
Phone: +44 1273 601041

#280
George Street Gallery
Category: Framing, Art Gallery
Address: 4 George Street
Brighton BN2 1RH, UK
Phone: +44 1273 681852

#281
The Palace of Fun Amusement Arcade
Category: Arcade, Amusement Parks
Address: Madeira Dr
Brighton BN2 1TW, UK

#282
Artscape
Category: Graffiti Artists
Address: Artscape Project.
Brighton BN1, UK

#283
Brighton Comedy Festival
Category: Comedy Club, Performing Arts
Address: 29 New Rd
Brighton BN1 1UG, UK
Phone: +44 1273 709709

#284
Academy Of Creative Training
Category: Performing Arts
Address: 8-10 Rock Place
Brighton BN2 1PF, UK
Phone: +44 1273 818266

#285
Cub Culture
Category: Art Gallery
Address: 28 York Place Studio
Brighton BN1 4GU, UK

#286
Acaster Langridge
Category: Art Gallery
Address: 243 Kings Rd Arches
Brighton BN1 1NB, UK

#287
Brighton Fishing Quarter Gallery
Category: Local Flavor, Art Gallery
Average price: Modest
Address: Brighton Fishing Quarter
Brighton BN1 1NB, UK

#288
Gamer Heaven
Category: Arcade
Address: 124 Lewes Road
Brighton BN2 3LG, UK

#289
JAG Studio & Gallery
Category: Art Gallery
Average price: Modest
Address: 283A Madeira Dr
Brighton BN2 1PT, UK
Phone: +44 7810 523984

#290
The Nightingale Theatre
Category: Performing Arts, Music Venues
Address: 29-30 Surrey Street
Brighton BN1 3PA, UK
Phone: +44 1273 702563

#291
Mint Casino Brighton
Category: Casino
Address: 6-8 Preston Street
Brighton BN1 2HN, UK
Phone: +44 1273 725101

#292
Sussex Beer Festival
Category: Festival
Address: Hove Town Hall
Brighton BN3 4AH, UK

#293
Monte Carlo Nights
Category: Casino
Address: 16 Hornby Road
Brighton BN2 4JL, UK
Phone: +44 1273 701715

#294
Eclectia
Category: Art Gallery
Address: 3 Mermaid Walk
Brighton BN2 5WA, UK
Phone: +44 7734 593393

#296
24 Hour Museum
Category: Museum
Address: 5 Frederick Terrace
Brighton BN1 1AX, UK
Phone: +44 1273 623266

#297
The Red Rooms
Category: Bar, Music Venues
Address: 8 Queens Road
Brighton BN1 3WA, UK

#298
The Blue Man
Category: African, Moroccan, Jazz & Blues
Average price: Modest
Address: 8 Queens Road
Brighton BN1 3WA, UK
Phone: +44 1273 726003

#299
Bigart
Category: Art Gallery
Address: 73 Trafalgar Street
Brighton BN1 4EB, UK
Phone: +44 1273 606044

#300
Big Art
Category: Art Gallery
Address: 73 Trafalgar Street
Brighton BN1 4EB, UK
Phone: +44 1273 606044

#301
Ambience Gallery
Category: Art Gallery
Address: 38 Meeting House Ln
Brighton BN1 1HB, UK
Phone: +44 1273 776607

#302
Nobles Amusements
Category: Arcade
Address: 10 London Rd
Brighton BN1 4JH, UK
Phone: +44 1273 604375

#303
First Light
Category: Art Gallery
Address: 3 Nile Street
Brighton BN1 1HW, UK
Phone: +44 1273 327344

#304
Hush Art Cafe
Category: Art Gallery
Address: Castle St
Brighton BN1 2HW, UK
Phone: +44 1273 772427

#305
Ali Cats
Category: Music Venues, Jazz & Blues, Pub
Average price: Inexpensive
Address: 80 East Street
Brighton BN1 1NF, UK
Phone: +44 1273 048103

#306
Margaret's
Category: Psychics & Astrologers
Address: 64 Elm Grove
Brighton BN2 3DD, UK
Phone: +44 1273 683623

#307
The Basement Arts Production, South East
Category: Cultural Center
Address: Argus Lofts
Brighton BN1 4AJ, UK
Phone: +44 1273 699733

#308
Jeremy Sanders
Category: Art Gallery
Address: 237 Kings Road Arches
Brighton BN1 1NB, UK
Phone: +44 1273 777340

#309
Angel World
Category: Psychics & Astrologers
Address: 5 Brighton Pl
Brighton BN1 1HJ, UK
Phone: +44 1273 728398

#310
Paul Hughes Barlow
Category: Psychics & Astrologers
Address: 261 Kings Road Arches
Brighton BN2 1TD, UK
Phone: +44 7918 637940

#311
Captain Corri's Card Club
Category: Social Club
Address: 178 Church Rd
Brighton BN3 2DJ, UK
Phone: +44 1273 736420

#312
Framework
Category: Art Gallery
Average price: Modest
Address: 26 Kensington Gardens
Brighton BN1 4AL, UK
Phone: +44 1273 818585

#313
Monarch Amusements
Category: Arcade
Address: 38 London Rd
Brighton BN1 4JB, UK

#314
Silver Streak Amusments
Category: Arcade
Address: 97 St James's Street
Brighton BN2 1TP, UK
Phone: +44 1273 670967

#315
Caia Matheson Artist
Category: Art Gallery
Average price: Modest
Address: Beaconsfield Studio
Brighton BN1 4QL, UK
Phone: +44 7961 405351

#316
Add the Colour
Category: Coffee & Tea, Art Gallery
Average price: Inexpensive
Address: 64-65 North Road
Brighton BN1 1YD, UK
Phone: +44 7817 850202

#317
Edited
Category: Home Decor, Furniture Stores, Art Gallery
Address: 3 Gardner Street
Brighton BN1 1UP, UK
Phone: +44 1273 604006

#318
No Walls Gallery
Category: Art Gallery
Address: 114 Church Street
Brighton BN1 1UD, UK
Phone: +44 1273 324432

#319
Above the Hobgoblin Venue
Category: DJs, Music Venues
Average price: Inexpensive
Address: 31 York Street
Brighton BN1 4GU, UK
Phone: +44 7891 965045

#320
Sascha Cooper
Category: Psychics & Astrologers
Address: 43 Providence Place
Brighton BN1 4GE, UK
Phone: +44 7912 650317

#321
Richard Whadcock
Category: Art Gallery, Cultural Center
Address: 10-14 Waterloo Place
Brighton BN2 9NB, UK
Phone: +44 7726 342610

#322
The Verdict
Category: Jazz & Blues
Average price: Inexpensive
Address: 159 Edward Street
Brighton BN2 0JB, UK
Phone: +44 1273 674847

#323
Chocolate Courses
Category: Social Club
Address: 01 Pelham Street
Brighton BN1, UK
Phone: +44 7446 300786

#324
Cloud Gallery
Category: Art Gallery
Address: 18 Brighton Place
Brighton BN1 1HJ, UK
Phone: +44 7917 886477

#325
Phoenix Community Centre
Category: Cultural Center
Address: 2 Phoenix Place
Brighton BN2 9ND, UK
Phone: +44 1273 621794

#326
Kukizu
Category: Performing Arts, Kids Activities
Address: 85-87 Holland Road
Brighton BN3 1JP, UK
Phone: +44 1273 732926

#327
Makers Boutique
Category: Arts & Crafts, Arts & Entertainment
Address: st nicholas church
Brighton BN1 3GD, UK

#328
Jilted Dog Gallery
Category: Art Gallery
Address: 46 New England Road
Brighton BN1 4GG, UK
Phone: +44 4479 4644 4296

#329
Mechanical Memories
Category: Museum
Address: 250C King's Road Arches
Brighton BN1 1NB, UK

#330
Brighton Festival Chorus
Category: Performing Arts
Average price: Modest
Address: Pavilion Buildings
Brighton BN1 1EE, UK
Phone: +44 7010 706235

#331
Brighton Dome
Category: Performing Arts, Music Venues
Average price: Expensive
Address: Church Street
Brighton BN1, UK
Phone: +44 1273 700747

#332
Speigletent
Category: Performing Arts
Address: Old Steine
Brighton BN1, UK

#333
KooKlub
Category: Nightclub, Social Club
Address: 10 Pool Valley
Brighton BN1 1NJ, UK
Phone: +44 1723 888000

#334
Suzart
Category: Art Gallery
Address: 280 Suzart at the Jag Gallery
Brighton BN2, UK
Phone: +44 7530 672888

#335
Bacchus
Category: Wholesale Stores, Wineries
Address: 2 Coombe Road
Brighton BN2 4FL, UK
Phone: +44 7846 370116

#337
Gay Figure Paintings @ Gulliver's
Category: Festival
Address: Gulliver's Hotel 12a New Steine,
Brighton BN2 1PB, UK
Phone: +44 7919 505206

#338
Coach House in Kemptown
Category: Art Gallery
Address: 22 Walpole Road
Brighton BN2 0EA, UK

#339
Kemp Town Carnival
Category: Festival
Address: St Georges Road
Brighton BN2 1ED, UK

#340
Thomas Rainsford Professional Picture Framing
Category: Framing, Art Supplies,
Address: 8 Arundel Mews
Brighton BN2 1GG, UK
Phone: +44 1273 689699

#341
Fishtail Neon
Category: Art Gallery
Address: 282 Madeira Drive Arches
Brighton BN2 1EN, UK

#343
My Big Fat Brighton Weekend
Category: Party & Event Planning
Address: 6 Chesham Street
Brighton BN2 1NA, UK
Phone: +44 1273 523966

#346
Brighton Marina Hand Car Wash & Valeting Service
Category: Parking, Cinema
Address: Brighton Marina Village
Brighton BN2 5UF, UK
Phone: +44 7799 418471

#348
Brighton Drama School
Category: Kids Activities
Address: Lewes Rd Brighton, UK
Phone: +44 1273 628549

#349
Sussex Masonic Centre
Category: Social Club
Address: 25 Queens Road
Brighton BN1 3YH, UK
Phone: +44 1273 325917

#350
Big Love Records
Category: Arcade
Address: 54 Buckingham Road
Brighton BN1 3RQ, UK
Phone: +44 1273 220859

#351
Aktivator
Category: Arcade
Address: 45a Trafalgar Street
Brighton BN1 4ED, UK
Phone: +44 1273 686877

#352
Hartline
Category: Performing Arts
Address: 14 Hampton Place
Brighton BN1 3DD, UK
Phone: +44 1273 720783

#353
Benedict Geddis
Category: Psychics & Astrologers
Address: 10a Montpelier Terrace
Brighton BN1 3DF, UK
Phone: +44 1273 220702

#354
Brighton Artists Gallery
Category: Art Gallery, Bar
Address: 108a Dyke Road
Brighton BN1 3TE, UK
Phone: +44 1273 711016

#355
Start Gallery
Category: Art Gallery
Address: 8 Church Street
Brighton BN1 1US, UK
Phone: +44 1273 233984

#356
Clairmonte Gallery
Category: Art Gallery
Address: 56 Gardner St
Brighton BN1 1UN, UK
Phone: +44 1273 622027

#357
O Contemporary
Category: Art Gallery
Address: 80 Trafalgar Street
Brighton BN1 4EB, UK
Phone: +44 1273 698500

#358
First Column Manangement
Category: Performing Arts
Address: 34 West Street
Brighton BN1 2RE, UK
Phone: +44 1273 724710

#359
Stars & Stripes
Category: Social Club
Address: 135 Western Road
Brighton BN1 2LA, UK
Phone: +44 1273 293340

#360
Yes No Productions
Category: Performing Arts
Address: 38 Ship Street
Brighton BN1 1AB, UK
Phone: +44 1273 736555

#361
Rarekind Art Gallery
Category: Art Gallery, Pub
Address: 102 North Road
Brighton BN1 1YE, UK
Phone: +44 1273 818170

#362
Brighton Fresh Design Solutions
Category: Professional Services
Address: 7 Gloucester Yard
Brighton BN1 4AF, UK
Phone: +44 7818 052378

#363
Quod Art
Category: Art Gallery
Address: 160 North Street
Brighton BN1 1EZ, UK
Phone: +44 1273 772002

#364
A L T Records
Category: Performing Arts
Address: 7 Old Shoreham Road
Brighton BN1 5DQ, UK
Phone: +44 1273 711749

#365
Bros Entertainment Merchandising
Category: Performing Arts
Address: 27 Old Shoreham Road
Brighton BN1 5DQ, UK
Phone: +44 1273 739124

#366
Best of Sussex
Category: Art Gallery
Address: 30 New Road
Brighton BN1 1BN, UK

#367
Stanley International Casino
Category: Social Club, Casino
Address: 6-8 Preston Street
Brighton BN1 2HN, UK
Phone: +44 1273 725101

#368
The ONCA Gallery
Category: Art Gallery
Address: 14 St George's Place
Brighton BN1 4GB, UK
Phone: +44 1273 958291

#369
Positive Productions
Category: Performing Arts
Address: 50 Providence Place
Brighton BN1 4GE, UK
Phone: +44 1273 681234

#370
Window Gallery
Category: Art Gallery
Address: Dyke Road
Brighton BN1 3JD, UK
Phone: +44 1273 726190

#371
Open Studio
Category: Arts & Crafts
Address: 168 Kings Rd Arches
Brighton BN1 1NB, UK
Phone: +44 1273 725013

#372
10 Below
Category: Jazz & Blues
Address: 10 Ship Street
Brighton BN1 1AD, UK
Phone: +44 1273 328439

#373
Good Company Theatre
Category: Performing Arts
Address: Powis Road
Brighton BN1 3HJ, UK
Phone: +44 1273 779955

#374
Bystander Shisha Lounge
Category: Lounge, Music Venues
Address: 35 London Road
Brighton BN1 4JB, UK
Phone: +44 7500 696996

#375
Betfred
Category: Casino
Address: 55 London Road
Brighton BN1 4JE, UK

#376
The Artist Quarter
Category: Art Gallery
Address: Kings Road Arches
Brighton BN1 1NS, UK

#377
Brighton & Hove Chinese Society
Category: Social Club
Address: 149 Western Road
Brighton BN1 2DD, UK
Phone: +44 1273 721723

#378
Dreamthinkspeak
Category: Performing Arts
Address: Flat 2 79 Rose Hill Terrace
Brighton BN1 4JL, UK
Phone: +44 1273 680159

#379
Brighton Fringe Arts Production
Category: Performing Arts
Address: Kensington Street
Brighton BN1 4AJ, UK
Phone: +44 1273 688677

#380
Basement South East
Category: Social Club
Address: Kensington Street
Brighton BN1 4AJ, UK
Phone: +44 1273 699733

#381
Surrounds
Category: Art Gallery
Address: 8 Little East Street
Brighton BN1 1HT, UK
Phone: +44 1273 327843

#382
Actors Of Dionysus
Category: Performing Arts
Address: 44-46 Old Steine
Brighton BN1 1NH, UK
Phone: +44 1273 320396

#383
Aod
Category: Performing Arts
Address: 44-46 Old Steine
Brighton BN1 1NH, UK
Phone: +44 1273 320395

#384
Project
Category: Nightclub, Music Venues
Address: West Street
Brighton BN1 1AZ, UK
Phone: +44 1273 321628

#385
Smiles Entertainment
Category: Arcade
Address: 79 Ditchling Road
Brighton BN1 4SD, UK
Phone: +44 1273 622022

#386
Art Pool Gallery
Category: Art Gallery
Address: 2 Pool Valley
Brighton BN1 1NJ, UK
Phone: +44 1273 777887

#387
Shift
Category: Performing Arts
Address: 47 Stanley Road
Brighton BN1 4NH, UK
Phone: +44 1273 606465

#388
Brighton & Hove Philharmonic Society
Category: Performing Arts
Address: 41 George Street
Brighton BN2 1RJ, UK
Phone: +44 1273 622900

#389
Waap Event Services
Category: Performing Arts
Address: 9-12 Middle Street
Brighton BN1 1AL, UK
Phone: +44 1273 777272

#390
The Copy Room
Category: Performing Arts
Address: 73A Shipwrights Yard
Brighton BN1 1AL, UK
Phone: +44 1273 777382

#391
Big I Am Productions
Category: Performing Arts
Address: 5 New England House
Brighton BN1 4GH, UK
Phone: +44 1273 605511

#392
Appetite
Category: Performing Arts
Address: 2 Coventry Street
Brighton BN1 5PQ, UK
Phone: +44 1273 888099

#393
Secrets Club
Category: Social Club
Address: 5 Steine Street
Brighton BN2 1TE, UK
Phone: +44 1273 609672

#394
Bighton Projects
Category: Performing Arts
Address: 22 Charles Street
Brighton BN2 1TG, UK
Phone: +44 1273 601004

#395
White Night
Category: Festival
Address: Old Steine
Brighton BN1 1, UK
Phone: +44 7505 003026

#396
The Show Team Productions
Category: Arcade
Address: 18 Windmill Street
Brighton BN2 0GN, UK
Phone: +44 1273 671010

#397
Hanover Productions
Category: Arcade
Address: The Stablehouse 73
Hanover Street, Brighton BN2 9SS, UK
Phone: +44 1273 606475

#398
Royal British Legion
Category: Social Club
Address: 39-40 ST. James's Street
Brighton BN2 1RG, UK
Phone: +44 1273 691365

#399
Artist Quarter Under the Arches
Category: Irish, Art Gallery
Address: 280 - Brighton BN2 1WP, UK

#400
The Puppeteers Co
Category: Performing Arts
Address: PO Box 350
Brighton BN2 1TZ, UK
Phone: +44 1273 687183

#401
Melting Vinyl
Category: Performing Arts
Address: Old Steine
Brighton BN1 1EJ, UK
Phone: +44 1273 685758

#402
Mahoney & Gretton Associates
Category: Performing Arts
Address: 18 Margaret Street
Brighton BN2 1TS, UK
Phone: +44 1273 685970

#403
The White Eagle Lodge
Category: Social Club, Health & Medical
Address: 15 Park Crescent Road
Brighton BN2 3HF, UK
Phone: +44 1273 626111

#404
Passe-Partout
Category: Performing Arts
Address: 13 Stanford Avenue
Brighton BN1 6AD, UK
Phone: +44 1273 557595

#405
Abigail
Category: Psychics & Astrologers
Address: 19 Grant Street
Brighton BN2 9UN, UK
Phone: +44 1273 270925

#406
Lumenessence
Category: Performing Arts
Address: 103 Islingword Road
Brighton BN2 9SG, UK
Phone: +44 1273 701997

#407
Gallery 73
Category: Art Gallery, Arts & Crafts
Address: 73 St James St
Brighton BN2 1PJ, UK

#408
P Mirza
Category: Psychics & Astrologers
Address: 216 Kings Road Arches
Brighton BN1 1NB, UK
Phone: +44 1273 721859

#409
N Emery
Category: Art Gallery
Address: 231 Kings Road Arches
Brighton BN1 1NB, UK
Phone: +44 1273 735927

#410
Gilburt
Category: Art Gallery
Address: Madeira Drive
Brighton BN2 1PS, UK
Phone: +44 1273 621777

#411
A O D
Category: Performing Arts
Address: 14 Cuthbert Road
Brighton BN2 0EN, UK
Phone: +44 1273 692604

#412
Ooosh! Tours
Category: Party Equipment Rentals, Music Venues
Address: Enterprise Point
Brighton BN2 3LH, UK
Phone: +44 1273 767155

#413
Brighton Trades Labour Club & Institute
Category: Social Club
Address: 164-166 Elm Grove
Brighton BN2 3DA, UK
Phone: +44 1273 681784

#414
Muse Fine Art & Design
Category: Art Gallery
Address: 12 Newmarket Road
Brighton BN2 3QF, UK
Phone: +44 1273 671450

#415
Jerkin Crocus Promotions
Category: Arcade
Address: 87 Roedale Road
Brighton BN1 7GD, UK
Phone: +44 1273 706090

#416
Ultima Hora Travel
Category: Performing Arts
Address: 4 Seymour Square
Brighton BN2 1DP, UK
Phone: +44 1273 621522

#417
Ikon Gallery
Category: Art Gallery
Address: 3 Albany Mews
Brighton BN3 2PQ, UK
Phone: +44 1273 775630

#418
Sijale Exposure Co
Category: Performing Arts
Address: 150 Donald Hall Road
Brighton BN2 5DJ, UK
Phone: +44 7899 786367

#419
Seven Veils Productions
Category: Dance Schools, Performing Arts, Dance Studio
Address: 14 Chesham Place
Brighton BN2 1FB, UK
Phone: +44 1273 885585

#420
Art Asylum
Category: Art Gallery
Address: 14a Chesham Road
Brighton BN2 1NB, UK
Phone: +44 1273 626426

#421
Elite Music Management
Category: Arcade
Address: 68 Baden Road
Brighton BN2 4DP, UK
Phone: +44 1273 621999

#422
Brighton Mini Club
Category: Social Club
Address: 15 Pulborough Close
Brighton BN2 5QT, UK
Phone: +44 1273 242505

#423
Whitehawk & Manor Farm Community Association
Category: Social Club
Address: Whitehawk Way
Brighton BN2 5HE, UK
Phone: +44 1273 673792

#424
Jennie Ricketts
Category: Art Gallery
Address: Arundel Place
Brighton BN2 1GG, UK
Phone: +44 1273 605070

#425
Moulsecoomb Social Club
Category: Social Club
Address: Moulsecoomb Place
Brighton BN2 4GA, UK
Phone: +44 1273 681156

#426
S Ainsworth
Category: Museum
Address: 17 Courcels Arundel Street
Brighton BN2 5UB, UK
Phone: +44 1273 673907

#427
Brighton Marina Yacht Club
Category: Performing Arts
Address: Brighton Marina Yacht Club Ltd,
Brighton BN2 5UT, UK
Phone: +44 1273 818711

#428
D Summers
Category: Psychics & Astrologers
Address: 13 Rotherfield Crescent
Brighton BN1 8FF, UK
Phone: +44 1273 562495

#429
Hove Museum & Art Gallery
Category: Museum, Local Flavor
Address: 19 New Church Road
Hove BN3 4AB, UK
Phone: +44 30 0029 0200

#430
Dukes @ Komedia
Category: Cinema
Address: 44-47 Gardner Street
Brighton and Hove BN1 1UN, UK

#431
Church Of Christ The King
Category: Churches, Social Club
Address: 21-23 Clarendon Villas
Hove BN3 3RE, UK
Phone: +44 1273 747687

#432
Coral
Brighton & Hove
Greyhound Stadium
Category: Stadiums & Arenas
Address: Nevill Road
Hove BN3 7BZ, UK
Phone: +44 1273 204601

#433
Naked Eye
Category: Art Gallery
Average price: Modest
Address: 5 Farm Mews
Hove BN3 1GH, UK
Phone: +44 1273 204800

#434
Greenhouse Effect
Category: Pub, Music Venues
Average price: Modest
Address: 63 Church Road
Hove BN3 2BD, UK
Phone: +44 1273 204783

#435
Neptune Inn
Category: Pub, Music Venues
Average price: Modest
Address: 10 Victoria Terrace
Hove BN3 2WB, UK
Phone: +44 1273 736390

#436
British Engineerium
Category: Museum
Address: The Droveway
Hove BN3 7QA, UK

#437
Cineworld
Category: Cinema
Address: Park Square
Brighton Marina Village BN2 5UF, UK
Phone: +44 871 200 2000

#438
Taylor Made Frames
Category: Art Gallery
Address: 3 Brighton Square
Brighton and Hove BN3 1HD, UK
Phone: +44 1273 739409

#439
Heavy Artillery - Antiques Roadshow Murial
Category: Local Flavor
Address: Seven Dials
Brighton BN1 3TD, UK

#440
Brighton Station Graffiti Wall
Category: Local Flavor, Graffiti Artists
Address: Brighton Station
Brighton and Hove BN1 3XP, UK

#441
Grosvenor Casino
Category: Casino
Address: Albany Mews
Hove BN3 2PQ, UK
Phone: +44 1273 720261

#443
The Blind Tiger Club
Category: Music Venues
Average price: Inexpensive
Address: 52 - 54 Grand Parade
Brighton BN2 9QA, UK
Phone: +44 1273 688869

#444
One Eyed Jacks
Category: Art Gallery
Address: 28 York Place
North Laine BN1 4GU, UK
Phone: +44 7743 098530

#445
The Ranelagh
Category: Jazz & Blues
Address: 2-3 high street
Brighton BN2 1RP, UK
Phone: +44 1273 681634

#446
I Love Jools
Category: Adult Education
Address: 5 Landseer Road
Hove BN3 7AF, UK
Phone: +44 1273 724949

#447
Gala Bingo
Category: Arcade
Address: 193 Portland Road
Hove BN3 5JB, UK
Phone: +44 1273 733985

#448
Caricature Shack
Category: Party Supplies
Address: 2 heath field Avenue
Hove BN2 4FH, UK
Phone: +44 7930 150001

#449
Arthouse Gallery
Category: Art Gallery
Address: 10 Western Road
Hove BN3 1AE, UK
Phone: +44 1273 770083

#450
Polish Community Centre
Category: Social Club
Address: 78 Farm Road
Hove BN3 1FD, UK
Phone: +44 1273 205864

TOP 450 NIGHTLIFE

Recommended by Locals & Trevelers

(From #1 to #450)

#1
Riddle & Finns
Category: Seafood, Champagne Bar
Average price: Expensive
Address: 12 Meeting House Lane
Brighton BN1 1HB, UK
Phone: +44 1273 721667

#2
The Lion & Lobster
Category: Pub
Average price: Modest
Address: 24 Silwood Street
Brighton BN1 2PS, UK
Phone: +44 1273 327299

#3
Bom-Bane's
Category: Coffee & Tea,
Music Venues, Belgian
Average price: Expensive
Address: 24 George Street
Brighton BN2 1RH, UK
Phone: +44 1273 606400

#4
Concorde 2
Category: Nightclub,
Bar, Music Venues
Average price: Modest
Address: Madeira Drive
Brighton BN2 1EN, UK
Phone: +44 1273 673311

#5
Northern Lights
Category: Scandinavian, Pub
Average price: Modest
Address: 6 Little E Street
Brighton BN1 1HT, UK
Phone: +44 1273 747096

#6
Hand In Hand
Category: Pub
Average price: Expensive
Address: 33 Upper ST James's Street
Brighton BN2 1JN, UK
Phone: +44 1273 699595

#7
Hop Poles
Category: Pub, British
Average price: Modest
Address: 13 Middle Street
Brighton BN1 1AL, UK
Phone: +44 1273 207566

#8
The Bee's Mouth
Category: Pub
Average price: Modest
Address: 10 Western Road
Brighton BN3 1AE, UK
Phone: +44 1273 770083

#9
Bath Arms
Category: Pub, British, Coffee & Tea
Average price: Modest
Address: 4 Meeting House Lane
Brighton BN1 1HB, UK
Phone: +44 1273 731864

#10
The Hop Poles
Category: Pub
Average price: Modest
Address: 13 Middle Street
Brighton BN1 1AL, UK
Phone: +44 1273 207566

#11
Lucky Voice Karaoke
Category: Karaoke, Bar, Pizza
Average price: Expensive
Address: 8 Black Lion Street
Brighton BN1 1ND, UK
Phone: +44 1273 715770

#12
Hotel Pelirocco
Category: Bar, Hotel, Music Venues
Average price: Expensive
Address: 10 Regency Square
Brighton BN1 2FG, UK
Phone: +44 1273 327055

#13
Brighton Festival Fringe
Category: Performing Arts,
Comedy Club
Average price: Modest
Address: 12a Pavilion Buildings
Brighton BN1 1EE, UK
Phone: +44 1273 260832

#14
The Windmill
Category: Pub, British
Average price: Modest
Address: 69 Upper North Street
Brighton BN1 3FL, UK
Phone: +44 1273 202475

#15
Barley Mow
Category: Pub
Average price: Modest
Address: 92 St Georges Road
Brighton BN2 1EE, UK
Phone: +44 1273 682259

#16
Robin Hood
Category: Pub
Average price: Modest
Address: 3 Norfolk Place
Brighton BN1 2PF, UK
Phone: +44 1273 325645

#17
Brighton Dome
Category: Performing Arts, Music Venues
Average price: Expensive
Address: Church Street
Brighton BN1, UK
Phone: +44 1273 700747

#18
Saint James
Category: Pub, Thai
Average price: Modest
Address: 16 Madeira Place
Brighton BN2 1TN, UK
Phone: +44 1273 626696

#19
The Prince George
Category: British, Pub, Vegetarian
Average price: Modest
Address: 5 Trafalgar Street
Brighton BN1 4EQ, UK
Phone: +44 1273 681055

#20
The Dorset
Category: Seafood, Pub
Average price: Modest
Address: 28 North Road
Brighton BN1 1YB, UK
Phone: +44 1273 605423

#21
Great Eastern
Category: Pub
Average price: Modest
Address: 103 Trafalgar Street
Brighton BN1 4ER, UK
Phone: +44 1273 685681

#22
The Greys
Category: Pub, British
Average price: Modest
Address: 105 Southover Street
Brighton BN2 9UA, UK
Phone: +44 1273 680734

#23
Audio
Category: Nightclub, Cocktail Bar
Average price: Modest
Address: 10 Marine Parade
Brighton BN2 1TL, UK
Phone: +44 1273 606906

#24
The Sidewinder
Category: Pub
Average price: Modest
Address: 65 Upper St James's Street
Brighton BN2 1JN, UK
Phone: +44 1273 679927

#25
Three Jolly Butchers
Category: Pub
Average price: Inexpensive
Address: 59 North Road
Brighton BN1 1YD, UK
Phone: +44 1273 608571

#26
Queens Arms
Category: Pub, Gay Bar, Karaoke
Average price: Modest
Address: 7 George Street
Brighton BN2 1RH, UK
Phone: +44 1273 696873

#27
Park Crescent
Category: Pub, British
Average price: Modest
Address: 39 Park Crescent Terrace
Brighton BN2 3HE, UK
Phone: +44 1273 604993

#28
Black Lion
Category: Pub, GastroPub, British
Average price: Modest
Address: 14 Black Lion Street
Brighton BN1 1ND, UK
Phone: +44 1273 711884

#29
Lord Nelson
Category: Pub
Average price: Modest
Address: 36 Trafalgar Street
Brighton BN1 4ED, UK
Phone: +44 1273 695872

#30
The Eagle
Category: Pub, British
Average price: Modest
Address: 125 Gloucester Road
Brighton BN1 4AF, UK
Phone: +44 1273 607765

#31
Fitzherberts
Category: Pub, Music Venues
Average price: Modest
Address: 25 New Road
Brighton BN1 1UG, UK
Phone: +44 1273 682401

#32
Earth And Stars
Category: GastroPub, Pub
Average price: Modest
Address: 46 Windsor Street
Brighton BN1 1RJ, UK
Phone: +44 1273 722879

#33
Funky Fish Bar & Club
Category: Nightclub, Bar
Average price: Modest
Address: 19 Marine Parade
Brighton BN2 1TL, UK
Phone: +44 1273 698331

#34
Pavilion Theatre Brighton
Category: Performing Arts, Music Venues
Address: New Road
Brighton BN1 1UG, UK
Phone: +44 1273 709709

#35
Waggon & Horses
Category: Pub, British
Average price: Modest
Address: 109 Church St
Brighton BN1 1UD, UK
Phone: +44 1273 602752

#36
Open House
Category: Pub, GastroPub
Average price: Modest
Address: 146 Springfield Road
Brighton BN1 6BZ, UK
Phone: +44 1273 880102

#37
The Colonnade
Category: Pub, Lounge
Average price: Modest
Address: 10 New Road
Brighton BN1 1UF, UK
Phone: +44 1273 328728

#38
Three and Ten
Category: Pub, Comedy Club, Music Venues
Average price: Modest
Address: 10 Steine Street
Brighton BN2 1TE, UK
Phone: +44 1273 609777

#39
The Cricketers
Category: Pub, British
Average price: Modest
Address: 15 Black Lion Street
Brighton BN1 1ND, UK
Phone: +44 1273 329472

#40
Havana
Category: Champagne Bar, Nightclub, European
Average price: Exclusive
Address: 32 Duke Street
Brighton BN1 1AG, UK
Phone: +44 1273 773388

#41
The Globe
Category: Pub, Lounge
Average price: Modest
Address: 77 Middle St
Brighton BN1 1AL, UK
Phone: +44 1273 770685

#42
The Fishbowl
Category: Pub
Average price: Modest
Address: 74 East Street
Brighton BN1 1HQ, UK
Phone: +44 1273 777505

#43
The Font & Firkin
Category: Pub, Sports Bar
Average price: Inexpensive
Address: Union Street
Brighton BN1 1HA, UK
Phone: +44 1273 747727

#44
The Crescent
Category: Pub
Average price: Modest
Address: 6 Clifton Hill
Brighton BN1 3HL, UK
Phone: +44 1273 205260

#45
Casablanca Jazz Club
Category: Jazz & Blues, Nightclub, Bar
Average price: Inexpensive
Address: 3 Middle Street
Brighton BN1 1AL, UK
Phone: +44 1273 321817

#46
The Chimney House
Category: GastroPub, Pub, British
Average price: Expensive
Address: 28 Upper Hamilton Road
Brighton BN1 5DF, UK
Phone: +44 1273 556708

#47
The Druids Arms
Category: Pub, Music Venues
Average price: Inexpensive
Address: 79-81 Ditchling Road
Brighton BN1 4SD, UK
Phone: +44 1273 680596

#48
Heart & Hand
Category: Pub
Average price: Modest
Address: 75 North Road
Brighton BN1 1YD, UK
Phone: +44 1273 683320

#49
The Quadrant
Category: Pub
Average price: Modest
Address: 12-13 North Street
Brighton BN1 3GJ, UK
Phone: +44 1273 733238

#50
Volks Bar & Club
Category: Bar, Nightclub
Average price: Modest
Address: 3 Madeira Drive
Brighton BN2 1PS, UK
Phone: +44 1273 682828

#51
The Ranelagh
Category: Jazz & Blues, Pub
Average price: Modest
Address: 2-3 The High Street
Brighton BN2 1RP, UK
Phone: +44 1273 681634

#52
Las Iguanas
Category: Lounge, Mexican, Brazilian
Average price: Modest
Address: 7-8 Jubilee Street
Brighton BN1 1GE, UK
Phone: +44 1273 573550

#53
The Mash Tun
Category: Pub, British
Average price: Modest
Address: 1 Church Street
Brighton BN1 1UE, UK
Phone: +44 1273 684951

#54
The Pond
Category: Thai, Pub
Average price: Modest
Address: 49 Gloucester Road
Brighton BN1 4AQ, UK
Phone: +44 1273 621400

#55
Cowley Club
Category: Music Venues
Average price: Modest
Address: 12 London Road
Brighton BN1 4JA, UK
Phone: +44 872 148 6259

#56
The Reservoir
Category: Pub, Lounge
Average price: Modest
Address: 1 Howard Road
Brighton BN2 9TP, UK
Phone: +44 1273 692484

#57
The Hope
Category: Music Venues, Lounge, Pub
Average price: Inexpensive
Address: 10-12 Queens Road
Brighton BN1 3WA, UK
Phone: +44 872 148 5838

#58
The Wick Inn
Category: Pub, Beer, Wine & Spirits
Average price: Modest
Address: 63 Western Rd
Brighton BN3 1JD, UK
Phone: +44 1273 736436

#59
The Foundry
Category: Pub
Average price: Modest
Address: 13-14 Foundry Street
Brighton BN1 4AT, UK
Phone: +44 1273 697014

#60
Brighton Tavern
Category: Pub
Address: 99-100 Gloucester Road
Brighton BN1 4AP, UK
Phone: +44 1273 680365

#61
Solera
Category: Spanish, Wine Bar
Average price: Modest
Address: 42 Sydney Street
Brighton BN1 4EP, UK
Phone: +44 1273 673966

#62
Prestonville Arms
Category: Pub
Average price: Modest
Address: 64 Hamilton Road
Brighton BN1 5DN, UK
Phone: +44 1273 701007

#63
Latest Music Bar
Category: Music Venues
Average price: Modest
Address: 14 - 17 Manchester Street
Brighton BN2 1TF, UK
Phone: +44 1273 687171

#64
Plateau
Category: Wine Bar, French
Average price: Expensive
Address: 1 Bartholomews
Brighton BN1 1HG, UK
Phone: +44 1273 733085

#65
The Marlborough
Category: Gay Bar, Cinema, Performing Arts
Address: 4 Princes Street
Brighton BN2 1RD, UK
Phone: +44 1273 570028

#66
Fountain Head
Category: Pub, GastroPub
Average price: Expensive
Address: 101-103 North Road
Brighton BN1 1YE, UK
Phone: +44 1273 628091

#67
The Hobgoblin
Category: Pub, Music Venues
Average price: Inexpensive
Address: 31 York Place
Brighton BN1 4GU, UK
Phone: +44 1273 682933

#68
Brighton Festival
Category: Performing Arts, Jazz & Blues, Festival
Address: 29 New Road
Brighton BN1 1UG, UK
Phone: +44 1273 700747

#69
The Office
Category: Pub, Thai
Average price: Expensive
Address: 8-9 Sydney Street
Brighton BN1 4EN, UK
Phone: +44 1273 609134

#70
Bar Valentino
Category: Bar
Average price: Expensive
Address: 7A New Road
Brighton BN1 1US, UK
Phone: +44 1273 727898

#71
Corn Exchange
Category: Performing Arts, Music Venues
Average price: Modest
Address: Church Street
Brighton BN1 1UE, UK
Phone: +44 1273 700747

#72
Sussex Yeoman
Category: Pub, British
Average price: Expensive
Address: 7 Guildford Road
Brighton BN1 3LU, UK
Phone: +44 1273 327985

#73
Druids Head
Category: Pub, GastroPub
Average price: Modest
Address: 9 Brighton Place
Brighton BN1 1HJ, UK
Phone: +44 1273 325490

#74
Funky Buddha Lounge
Category: Art Gallery, Nightclub
Average price: Modest
Address: Kings Road Arches
Brighton BN1 1FL, UK

#75
Battle Of Trafalgar
Category: Pub
Average price: Modest
Address: 34 Guildford Road
Brighton BN1 3LW, UK
Phone: +44 1273 327997

#76
Pump House
Category: Pub
Average price: Modest
Address: 45-46 Market Street
Brighton BN1 1HH, UK
Phone: +44 1273 827421

#77
The West Hill
Category: Pub
Average price: Inexpensive
Address: 67 Buckingham Pl
Brighton BN1 3PQ, UK
Phone: +44 1273 748849

#78
The Pull and Pump
Category: Pub
Average price: Modest
Address: 1-2 Clarence Gardens
Brighton BN1 2EG, UK
Phone: +44 1273 328263

#79
Fiddler's Elbow
Category: Irish, Pub
Average price: Modest
Address: 11 Boyces Street
Brighton BN1 1AN, UK
Phone: +44 1273 325850

#80
Pub with No Name
Category: Pub, GastroPub
Average price: Modest
Address: 58 Southover Street
Brighton BN2 9UF, UK
Phone: +44 1273 601419

#81
The Gladstone
Category: Pub, British, Music Venues
Average price: Inexpensive
Address: 123 Lewes Road
Brighton BN2 3QB, UK
Phone: +44 4412 7362 0888

#82
Circus Circus
Category: Pub, Thai
Average price: Modest
Address: 2 Preston Road
Brighton BN1 4QF, UK
Phone: +44 1273 620026

#83
Hanover
Category: Pub
Average price: Modest
Address: 242 Queens Park Road
Brighton BN2 9ZB, UK
Phone: +44 1273 679902

#84
Gemini Beach Bar
Category: Pub
Average price: Expensive
Address: 127 Kings Rd Arches
Brighton BN1 2FN, UK
Phone: +44 1273 327888

#85
Digital
Category: Nightclub, Music Venues
Average price: Expensive
Address: 187-193 Kings Rd Arches
Brighton BN1 1NB, UK
Phone: +44 1273 227763

#86
King & Queen
Category: Pub, British, Sports Bar
Average price: Inexpensive
Address: 13-17 Marlborough Place
Brighton BN1 1UB, UK
Phone: +44 1273 607207

#87
The Thomas Kemp
Category: Pub
Average price: Modest
Address: 8 St Georges Road
Brighton BN2 1EB, UK
Phone: +44 1273 683334

#88
Proud Cabaret Brighton
Category: Nightclub, Lounge, Music Venues
Average price: Modest
Address: 83 St Georges Road
Brighton BN2 1EF, UK
Phone: +44 1273 605789

#89
Oxygen
Category: Lounge
Average price: Inexpensive
Address: 74 West St
Brighton BN1 2RA, UK
Phone: +44 1273 727378

#90
Basketmakers Arms
Category: Pub, British, Food
Average price: Inexpensive
Address: 12 Gloucester Road
Brighton BN1 4AD, UK
Phone: +44 1273 689006

#91
Pub du Vin
Category: Pub
Average price: Exclusive
Address: Ship Street
Brighton BN1 1AD, UK
Phone: +44 845 365 4438

#92
Club Revenge
Category: Nightclub, Gay Bar
Average price: Modest
Address: 32-34 Old Steine
Brighton BN1 1EL, UK
Phone: +44 1273 606064

#93
Seven Stars
Category: Pub, GastroPub
Average price: Modest
Address: 27 Ship St
Brighton BN1 1AD, UK
Phone: +44 1273 258800

#94
Charles Street
Category: Gay Bar
Average price: Modest
Address: 8 Marine Parade
Brighton BN2 1TA, UK
Phone: +44 1273 624091

#95
Amsterdam
Category: Hotel, Gay Bar, Day Spas
Average price: Inexpensive
Address: 11-12 Marine Parade
Brighton BN2 1TL, UK
Phone: +44 1273 688825

#96
Fortune of War
Category: Pub, Lounge, British
Average price: Modest
Address: 157 Kings Road Arches
Brighton BN1 1NB, UK
Phone: +44 1273 205065

#97
Merkaba
Category: Bar
Average price: Exclusive
Address: 17 Jubilee Street
Brighton BN1 1GE, UK
Phone: +44 1273 900300

#98
Dover Castle
Category: Pub, Seafood
Average price: Expensive
Address: 43 Southover Street
Brighton BN2 9UE, UK
Phone: +44 1273 245338

#99
Princess Victoria
Category: Pub
Average price: Modest
Address: 22-23 Upper N St
Brighton BN1 3FG, UK
Phone: +44 1273 325491

#100
Legends
Category: Hotel, Gay Bar
Average price: Modest
Address: 31-34 Marine Parade
Brighton BN2 1TR, UK
Phone: +44 1273 624462

#101
Madame Geisha
Category: Asian Fusion, Nightclub
Average price: Modest
Address: 75 - 79 East St
Brighton BN1 1NF, UK
Phone: +44 1273 770847

#102
The Brighton Coalition
Category: Nightclub, Music Venues
Average price: Modest
Address: 171-181 Kings Rd Arches
Brighton BN1 1NB, UK
Phone: +44 1273 772842

#103
Misty's
Category: British, Lounge
Average price: Expensive
Address: 116 Church Rd
Brighton BN3 2EA, UK
Phone: +44 1273 220302

#104
The World's End
Category: Pub, Music Venues
Average price: Modest
Address: 60-61 London Road
Brighton BN1 4JE, UK
Phone: +44 1273 692311

#105
The Geese
Category: Pub
Average price: Expensive
Address: 16 Southover Street
Brighton BN2 9UA, UK
Phone: +44 1273 693491

#106
The Signalman
Category: Pub, GastroPub
Average price: Modest
Address: 76 Ditchling Rise
Brighton BN1 4QQ, UK
Phone: +44 1273 689783

#107
The Cuthbert Pub & Kitchen
Category: Pub
Average price: Modest
Address: 136 Freshfield Road
Brighton BN2 0BR, UK
Phone: +44 1273 699693

#108
Atlas Lounge
Category: British, Lounge
Average price: Modest
Address: 111 Western Road
Brighton BN1 2AA, UK
Phone: +44 871 951 1000

#109
The Rock
Category: Pub
Average price: Modest
Address: 7 Rock Street
Brighton BN2 1NF, UK
Phone: +44 1273 697054

#110
The White Rabbit
Category: Pub, British, GastroPub
Average price: Expensive
Address: 13 Kensington Gardens
Brighton BN1 4AL, UK
Phone: +44 1273 677655

#111
Good Companions
Category: Pub, GastroPub
Average price: Inexpensive
Address: 132 Dyke Road
Brighton BN1 3TE, UK
Phone: +44 1273 202062

#112
Brighton Rocks
Category: Pub, Lounge
Average price: Modest
Address: 6 Rock Place
Brighton BN2 1PF, UK
Phone: +44 1273 601139

#113
The Full Moon
Category: Pub
Average price: Modest
Address: 8 Boyces Street
Brighton BN1 1AN, UK
Phone: +44 1273 328074

#114
Duke Of Norfolk
Category: Pub
Average price: Modest
Address: 113-114 Western Rd
Brighton BN1 2AB, UK
Phone: +44 1273 726057

#115
Preston Park Tavern
Category: Pub
Average price: Expensive
Address: 88 Havelock Road
Brighton BN1 6GF, UK
Phone: +44 1273 542271

#116
Park View
Category: Pub, British
Average price: Modest
Address: 71 Preston Drove
Brighton BN1 6LD, UK
Phone: +44 1273 541663

#117
Grand Central
Category: Pub, GastroPub
Average price: Modest
Address: 29-30 Surrey Street
Brighton BN1 3PA, UK
Phone: +44 1273 329086

#118
Caxton Arms
Category: Pub
Address: 36 North Gardens
Brighton BN1 3LB, UK
Phone: +44 1273 725866

#120
Market Inn
Category: Pub
Average price: Expensive
Address: 1 Market Street
Brighton BN1 1HH, UK
Phone: +44 1273 329483

#121
The Warren
Category: Music Venues
Average price: Modest
Address: 48-50 Russell Place
Brighton BN1 2RG, UK
Phone: +44 7800 983290

#122
The Constant Service
Category: Pub, British
Average price: Modest
Address: 96 Islingword Rd
Brighton BN2 9, UK
Phone: +44 1273 607058

#123
The Bear
Category: Pub
Average price: Modest
Address: 109 Lewes Road
Brighton BN2 4AE, UK
Phone: +44 1273 608565

#124
Marine Tavern
Category: Pub, Gay Bar
Address: 13 Broad Street
Brighton BN2 1TJ, UK
Phone: +44 1273 681284

#125
Brighton Little Theatre
Category: Performing Arts, Music Venues
Average price: Inexpensive
Address: 9 Clarence Gardens
Brighton BN1 2EG, UK
Phone: +44 1273 777748

#126
Walmer Castle
Category: Pub
Average price: Modest
Address: 95 Queens Park Road
Brighton BN2 0GH, UK
Phone: +44 1273 682466

#127
Hare & Hounds
Category: Pub
Average price: Modest
Address: 75 London Road
Brighton BN1 4JF, UK
Phone: +44 1273 681163

#128
Caroline Of Brunswick
Category: Pub, British
Average price: Inexpensive
Address: 39 Ditchling Road
Brighton BN1 4SB, UK
Phone: +44 1273 624434

#129
The London Unity
Category: Pub
Average price: Inexpensive
Address: 131 Islingword Road
Brighton BN2 9SH, UK
Phone: +44 1273 609364

#130
Round Georges
Category: Pub
Average price: Modest
Address: 14-15 Sutherland Road
Brighton BN2 0EQ, UK
Phone: +44 1273 691833

#131
Western Front
Category: Pub, Social Club, British
Average price: Inexpensive
Address: 11 Cranbourne St
Brighton BN1 2RD, UK
Phone: +44 1273 725656

#132
The Hampton
Category: Pub, GastroPub
Average price: Modest
Address: 57 Upper North St
Brighton BN1 3FH, UK
Phone: +44 1273 731347

#133
Northern Tavern
Category: Pub
Average price: Modest
Address: 85 Ditchling Road
Brighton BN1 4SD, UK
Phone: +44 1273 571540

#134
Oceana
Category: Nightclub, Lounge
Average price: Expensive
Address: West St
Brighton BN1 2RE, UK
Phone: +44 845 296 8590

#135
The Station Pub
Category: Bar, Pizza
Average price: Expensive
Address: 100 Goldstone Villas
Brighton BN3 3RU, UK
Phone: +44 1273 733660

#136
More
Category: Music Venues, Wine Bar
Average price: Modest
Address: 98 Trafalgar Street
Brighton BN1 4ER, UK
Phone: +44 1273 693377

#137
Riki Tik
Category: Cocktail Bar
Average price: Modest
Address: 18A Bond Street
Brighton BN1 1RD, UK
Phone: +44 1273 683844

#138
The Cornerstone
Category: Pub, Caribbean
Average price: Inexpensive
Address: 2-6 Elm Grove
Brighton BN2 3DD, UK
Phone: +44 1273 691028

#139
William The Fourth
Category: Pub
Average price: Modest
Address: 4 Church Street
Brighton BN1 1UJ, UK
Phone: +44 1273 683365

#140
Life
Category: Nightclub
Average price: Expensive
Address: 159-161 Kings Road
Brighton BN1 1NB, UK
Phone: +44 1273 770505

#141
Smugglers
Category: Sports Bar
Average price: Modest
Address: 10 Ship Street
Brighton BN1 1AD, UK
Phone: +44 1273 328439

#142
Medusa Bar
Category: Pub, Wine Bar
Average price: Modest
Address: 20 Preston Street
Brighton BN1 2HN, UK
Phone: +44 1273 326408

#143
The Rose Hill Tavern
Category: Pub
Average price: Modest
Address: 70-71 Rose Hill Terrace
Brighton BN1 4JL, UK
Phone: +44 1273 607825

#144
Varsity
Category: Bar
Average price: Inexpensive
Address: 80 E Street
Brighton BN1 1NF, UK
Phone: +44 1273 748103

#145
The Hartington
Category: Pub, GastroPub
Average price: Modest
Address: 41 Whippingham Road
Brighton BN2 3PF, UK
Phone: +44 1273 682874

#146
The Brasserie
Category: Italian, Bar
Average price: Modest
Address: 15d The Village Square Shops
Brighton BN2 5WA, UK
Phone: +44 1273 818026

#147
Duke Of Wellington
Category: Pub
Average price: Modest
Address: 70 Upper Gloucester Road
Brighton BN1 3LQ, UK
Phone: +44 1273 327989

#148
The PV
Category: Pub
Address: 161 Edward Street
Brighton BN2 0JB, UK
Phone: +44 1273 687090

#149
The Hydrant
Category: Pub, Music Venues, Nightclub
Average price: Inexpensive
Address: 75 London Road
Brighton BN1 4JF, UK
Phone: +44 1273 608313

#150
Doctor Brightons
Category: Gay Bar
Average price: Modest
Address: 16-17 Kings Rd
Brighton BN1 1NE, UK
Phone: +44 1273 208113

#151
Queens Park
Category: Pub, Parks
Address: Queen Park Road
Brighton BN2 9ZA, UK

#152
Ottoman Shisha Bar
Category: Turkish, Hookah Bar
Average price: Modest
Address: 35-38 Lewes Road
Brighton BN2 3HQ, UK
Phone: +44 1273 605314

#153
Railway Bell
Category: Pub
Average price: Modest
Address: 26-27 Surrey Street
Brighton BN1 3PA, UK
Phone: +44 1273 326730

#154
Bristol Bar
Category: Pub
Average price: Modest
Address: Paston Place
Brighton BN2 1HA, UK
Phone: +44 1273 605687

#155
The Engine Room
Category: Music Venues, Nightclub
Average price: Modest
Address: 5 Preston St
Brighton BN1 2HX, UK
Phone: +44 1273 728999

#156
Ohso Social
Category: British, Coffee & Tea, Bar
Average price: Modest
Address: 250a Kings Rd Arches
Brighton BN1 1NB, UK
Phone: +44 1273 746067

#157
St Georges Church
Category: Music Venues
Average price: Modest
Address: St Georges Rd
Brighton BN2 1ED, UK
Phone: +44 1273 279448

#158
The Queen's Head
Category: Pub
Average price: Modest
Address: 69 Queens Road
Brighton BN1 3XD, UK
Phone: +44 1273 205800

#159
Sir Charles Napier
Category: Pub
Average price: Modest
Address: 50 Southover Street
Brighton BN2 9UE, UK
Phone: +44 1273 601413

#160
Wetherspoons
Category: Pub, British
Average price: Modest
Address: 20-22a West Street
Brighton BN1 2RE, UK
Phone: +44 1273 224690

#161
Pitcher and Piano
Category: Wine Bar
Average price: Modest
Address: 5 Kings Road
Brighton BN1 1NB, UK
Phone: +44 1273 749780

#162
Bedford Tavern
Category: Pub
Average price: Modest
Address: 30 Western Street
Brighton BN1 2PG, UK
Phone: +44 1273 739495

#163
Vavoom
Category: Gay Bar
Average price: Inexpensive
Address: 31 Old Steine
Brighton BN1 1EL, UK
Phone: +44 1273 603010

#164
Bulldog Tavern
Category: Pub, Gay Bar
Average price: Inexpensive
Address: 31 St James's Street
Brighton BN2 1RF, UK
Phone: +44 1273 684097

#165
The Zone
Category: Gay Bar, Lounge
Average price: Modest
Address: 33 St. James St
Brighton BN2 1RF, UK
Phone: +44 1273 682249

#166
Barefoot Café Bar
Category: Wine Bar
Address: 299 Madeira Dr
Brighton BN2 1EN, UK
Phone: +44 1273 672222

#167
Rat & Trumpet
Category: Sports Bar, Pub
Address: 82 Dyke Road
Brighton BN1 3JD, UK
Phone: +44 1273 721285

#168
Wetherspoons
Category: Pub
Average price: Inexpensive
Address: West Quay
Brighton BN2 5UT, UK

#169
Regency Tavern
Category: Pub
Average price: Modest
Address: 32-34 Russell Square
Brighton BN1 2EF, UK
Phone: +44 1273 325652

#170
Montpelier Public House
Category: Pub
Average price: Modest
Address: 7-8 Montpelier Place
Brighton BN1 3BF, UK
Phone: +44 1273 770916

#171
112 Church Street
Category: Pub
Average price: Modest
Address: 112 Church St
Brighton BN1 1UD, UK
Phone: +44 1273 606864

#172
The Chapel Royal
Category: Music Venues
Address: 164 North St
Brighton BN1 1, UK
Phone: +44 1273 328767

#173
The Loft
Category: Bar
Address: 10 Ship St
Brighton BN1 1AD, UK
Phone: +44 1273 328439

#174
The Temple Bar
Category: Pub
Average price: Expensive
Address: 122 Western Rd
Brighton BN3 1, UK
Phone: +44 1273 721501

#175
Krater Comedy Club
Category: Comedy Club
Average price: Modest
Address: Komedia, 44-47 Gardner St
Brighton BN1 1UN, UK
Phone: +44 845 293 8480

#176
The Dyke
Category: Pub
Average price: Expensive
Address: 218 Dyke Road
Brighton BN1 5AA, UK
Phone: +44 1273 555672

#177
The Setting Sun
Category: Pub, GastroPub
Average price: Modest
Address: 1 Windmill Street
Brighton BN2 0GN, UK
Phone: +44 1273 626192

#178
Camelford Arms
Category: Gay Bar
Average price: Modest
Address: 30-31 Camelford Street
Brighton BN2 1TQ, UK
Phone: +44 1273 603726

#179
Mitre Tavern
Category: Pub
Average price: Modest
Address: 13 Baker Street
Brighton BN1 4JN, UK
Phone: +44 1273 683173

#180
Prince of Wales
Category: Pub
Average price: Expensive
Address: 47 Clarence Sq
Brighton BN1 2ED, UK
Phone: +44 1273 324391

#181
Brighton Ballroom
Category: British, Music Venues
Address: 83 St Georges Rd
Brighton BN2 1EF, UK
Phone: +44 1273 605789

#182
Irish Folk Night
Category: Music Venues
Address: 13-14 Foundry St
Brighton BN1 4AT, UK
Phone: +44 1273 697014

#183
The Kitchen Bar
Category: Bar
Address: 36 Preston Street
Brighton BN1 2HP, UK

#184
The Mucky Duck
Category: Pub
Address: 7-9 Manchester Street
Brighton BN2 1TF, UK
Phone: +44 1273 601450

#185
The Squid
Category: Pub
Address: 78 Middle Street
Brighton BN1 1AL, UK
Phone: +44 1273 727114

#186
West Beach Rock Cafe
Category: Bar
Address: 135 Kings Road
Brighton BN1 2HX, UK
Phone: +44 7526 776660

#187
The North Laine Pub & Brewery
Category: Pub, Food
Average price: Modest
Address: 27 Gloucester Place
Brighton BN1 4AA, UK
Phone: +44 1273 683666

#188
Post & Telegraph
Category: Pub
Average price: Inexpensive
Address: 155-158 North Street
Brighton BN1, UK
Phone: +44 1273 827540

#189
Born Bad
Category: Music Venues
Address: Komedia, 44-47 Gardner St
Brighton BN1 1UN, UK
Phone: +44 1273 647100

#190
Brighton Music Hall
Category: Bar, Music Venues
Average price: Inexpensive
Address: 127 Kings Road Arches
Brighton BN1 2FN, UK
Phone: +44 1273 747287

#191
Royal Oak
Category: Pub, Sports Bar
Average price: Modest
Address: 46 St James's Street
Brighton BN2 1RG, UK
Phone: +44 1273 621093

#192
Foggs
Category: Pub
Address: 82 Dyke Rd
Brighton BN1 3JD, UK
Phone: +44 1273 721285

#193
Ganges
Category: Indian, Lounge
Average price: Modest
Address: 93 Church Rd
Brighton BN3 2BA, UK
Phone: +44 1273 728292

#194
The Foragers
Category: GastroPub, Pub, British
Average price: Modest
Address: 3 Stirling Place
Brighton BN3 3YU, UK
Phone: +44 1273 733134

#195
The Blind Busker
Category: Pub
Average price: Modest
Address: 77 Church Road
Brighton BN3 2BB, UK
Phone: +44 1273 749110

#196
The Lectern
Category: Pub
Average price: Modest
Address: 5 Pelham Terrece
Brighton BN1 4AF, UK
Phone: +44 1273 685258

#197
Preston Brewery Tap
Category: Pub, Sports Bar,
Music Venues
Address: 197 Preston Road
Brighton BN1 6SA, UK
Phone: +44 1273 508700

#198
Old Orleans
Category: American, Lounge
Average price: Modest
Address: 1-3 Prince Albert Street
Brighton BN1 1HE, UK
Phone: +44 1273 747000

#200
The Iron Duke
Category: Pub, Guest House, British
Average price: Modest
Address: 3 Waterloo Street
Brighton BN3 1AQ, UK
Phone: +44 1273 734806

#201
The Stoneham
Category: Pub, Pizza
Average price: Exclusive
Address: 153 Portland Road
Brighton BN3, UK
Phone: +44 1273 383840

#202
All Bar One
Category: Wine Bar, British
Average price: Modest
Address: 2-3 Pavilion Bldg
Brighton BN1 1EE, UK
Phone: +44 1273 207593

#203
Brighton Centre
Category: Music Venues, Performing Arts
Average price: Modest
Address: Kings Rd
Brighton BN1 2GR, UK
Phone: +44 1273 290131

#204
The Eclipse
Category: Pub
Address: 33 Montgomery St
Brighton BN3 5, UK
Phone: +44 1273 272212

#205
The Engineer
Category: Pub
Average price: Inexpensive
Address: 32 Argyle Road
Brighton BN1 4QB, UK
Phone: +44 1273 675787

#206
Om Cocktail Lounge & Spirit Loft
Category: Lounge
Address: 5 Steine Street
Brighton BN2 1TE, UK
Phone: +44 1273 607304

#207
Royal Standard
Category: Pub
Average price: Expensive
Address: 59 Queens Road
Brighton BN1 3XD, UK
Phone: +44 1273 772300

#208
Green Door Store
Category: Music Venues
Address: Units 2 3 4 Trafalgar Arches
Brighton BN1 3XP, UK
Phone: +44 7944 693214

#209
The Bright Helm
Category: Pub
Average price: Inexpensive
Address: 20-22 West St
Brighton BN1 2RE, UK
Phone: +44 1273 224690

#210
Crown & Anchor
Category: Pub
Average price: Inexpensive
Address: 213 Preston Road
Brighton BN1 6SA, UK
Phone: +44 1273 559494

#211
The Penthouse
Category: Nightclub, Music Venues, Lounge
Average price: Modest
Address: 1 Phoenix Pl
Brighton BN2 9ND, UK
Phone: +44 872 148 6028

#212
Xuma
Category: Music Venues
Average price: Modest
Address: 108a Dyke Road
Brighton BN1 3TE, UK
Phone: +44 4412 7372 4036

#213
Red Lion
Category: Pub
Address: 1 Hove Pl
Brighton BN3 2RG, UK
Phone: +44 1273 770034

#214
Square Bar-Restaurant
Category: Wine Bar, Lounge, Italian
Average price: Modest
Address: 79 Western Road
Brighton BN3 2JQ, UK
Phone: +44 1273 772777

#215
H-Bar
Category: Champagne Bar, Nightclub
Average price: Modest
Address: 16 Church Rd
Brighton BN3 2FL, UK
Phone: +44 1273 725890

#216
Martha Gunn
Category: Pub
Average price: Modest
Address: 100 Upper Lewes Road
Brighton BN2 3FE, UK
Phone: +44 1273 681671

#217
Prince Albert
Category: Pub, Nightclub, Music Venues
Average price: Modest
Address: 48 Trafalgar Street
Brighton BN1 4ED, UK
Phone: +44 1273 730499

#218
Duke Of Beaufort
Category: Pub
Average price: Inexpensive
Address: 175 Queens Park Road
Brighton BN2 9ZA, UK
Phone: +44 1273 625429

#219
Katarina Harvester
Category: British, Pub
Average price: Modest
Address: Village Square
Brighton BN2 5WD, UK
Phone: +44 1273 606268

#220
Golden Cannon
Category: Pub
Average price: Modest
Address: 20-21 ST Georges Road
Brighton BN2 1EB, UK
Phone: +44 1273 607544

#221
Master Mariner
Category: Pub
Address: Brighton Marina
Brighton BN2 5WA, UK
Phone: +44 1273 670634

#222
The Dugout
Category: Pizza, Sports Bar
Average price: Modest
Address: 106 Lewes Road
Brighton BN2 3QA, UK
Phone: +44 1273 622310

#223
The Prince Arthur
Category: Pub, British
Average price: Modest
Address: 38 Dean Street
Brighton BN1 3EG, UK
Phone: +44 1273 205797

#224
Chameleon
Category: Bar
Average price: Modest
Address: 61a Western Road
Brighton BN1, UK
Phone: +44 1273 733870

#225
The Mesmerist
Category: Pub
Address: Prince Albert Street
Brighton BN1 1, UK
Phone: +44 1273 823866

#227
Square Hotel
Category: Hotel, Bar
Average price: Modest
Address: 4 New Steine
Brighton BN2 1PB, UK
Phone: +44 1273 691777

#228
Cobden Arms
Category: Pub
Average price: Inexpensive
Address: 45-46 Cobden Road
Brighton BN2 9TJ, UK
Phone: +44 1273 707996

#229
The Florist
Category: Pub
Address: 22-23 Upper N St
Brighton BN1 3FG, UK
Phone: +44 1273 325491

#230
Chequers
Category: Pub, Music Venues
Address: 45 Preston Street
Brighton BN1 2HP, UK
Phone: +44 1273 220855

#231
The Hydrant
Category: Sports Bar, Music Venues
Average price: Modest
Address: 75 London Road
Brighton BN1 4JF, UK
Phone: +44 1273 608313

#232
The Honey Club
Category: Nightclub
Average price: Inexpensive
Address: 214 Kings Road
Brighton BN1 1NB, UK
Phone: +44 1273 202807

#233
Grosvenor Casino
Category: Casino
Address: 9 Grand Junction Road
Brighton BN1 1PP, UK
Phone: +44 1273 326514

#234
Horse & Groom
Category: Pub
Average price: Modest
Address: 129 Islingword Road
Brighton BN2 9SH, UK
Phone: +44 1273 606546

#235
Franklin Tavern
Category: Pub, Sports Bar
Average price: Inexpensive
Address: 158 Lewes Road
Brighton BN2 3LF, UK
Phone: +44 1273 271152

#236
Sportsman Brewers Fayre
Category: Pub
Average price: Inexpensive
Address: Tongdean Lane
Brighton BN1 5JD, UK
Phone: +44 1273 330055

#237
The Albion
Category: Sports Bar, Pub
Average price: Inexpensive
Address: 110 Church Road
Brighton BN3 2EB, UK
Phone: +44 1273 772929

#238
Karma
Category: Pub
Average price: Modest
Address: 5 Waterfront
Brighton BN2 5WA, UK
Phone: +44 1273 818000

#239
Belushi's
Category: Sports Bar, Pub
Average price: Modest
Address: 10-12 Grand Junction Rd
Brighton BN1 1PN, UK
Phone: +44 1273 202035

#240
Rileys American Pool & Snooker Club
Category: Pool Halls
Average price: Modest
Address: 119 London Road
Brighton BN1 4JH, UK
Phone: +44 1273 604375

#241
Como Brasserie
Category: Bar, Brasseries
Address: 41 Market Street
Brighton BN1 1HH, UK
Phone: +44 1273 945045

#242
Loop
Category: Local Flavor, Music Venues
Address: 12A Pavilion Buildings
Brighton BN1 1EE, UK
Phone: +44 1273 700747

#244
Royal York Hotel
Category: Cocktail Bar
Address: Royal York Bld Old Steine
Brighton BN1 1NH, UK
Phone: +44 1273 766700

#245
The Funfair Club
Category: Nightclub
Average price: Expensive
Address: 12-15 Kings Road
Brighton BN1 1NE, UK

#246
Lola Lo
Category: Bar
Address: 75-79 East St
Brighton BN1 1NF, UK
Phone: +44 1273 777904

#247
The Prodigal
Category: Pub
Address: Clarendon Mansions East Street,
Brighton BN1 1NF, UK
Phone: +44 1273 748103

#248
Pussy Parlure
Category: Bar
Address: Old Steine
Brighton BN1 1, UK

#249
Brighton Comedy Festival
Category: Comedy Club,
Performing Arts
Address: 29 New Rd
Brighton BN1 1UG, UK
Phone: +44 1273 709709

#250
The Southover
Category: Bar
Address: 58 Southover Street
Brighton BN2 9UF, UK
Phone: +44 1273 601419

#251
The Niche
Category: Bar
Address: 2 Lower Rock Gardens
Brighton BN2 1PE, UK

#252
Bugle Inn
Category: Pub
Average price: Modest
Address: 24 ST. Martins Street
Brighton BN2 3HJ, UK
Phone: +44 1273 607753

#253
Southwick Beer Festival
Category: Bar
Address: Southwick Community Centre
Brighton BN1 1FL, UK
Phone: +44 1273 592819

#254
Kulture
Category: Nightclub, Lounge
Average price: Inexpensive
Address: 77 West Street
Brighton BN1 2RA, UK
Phone: +44 1273 227592

#255
Pasha
Category: Bar
Average price: Inexpensive
Address: 62 West Street
Brighton BN1 2RA, UK
Phone: +44 1273 771010

#256
The Eddy
Category: Pub, British
Address: 67a Upper Gloucester Road
Brighton BN1 3LQ, UK
Phone: +44 1273 329540

#258
The Nightingale Theatre
Category: Performing Arts,
Music Venues
Address: 29-30 Surrey Street
Brighton BN1 3PA, UK
Phone: +44 1273 702563

#259
The Aquarium
Category: Gay Bar
Average price: Inexpensive
Address: 6 Steine Street
Brighton BN2 1TE, UK
Phone: +44 1273 605525

#260
Entourage
Category: Nightclub, Champagne Bar
Average price: Modest
Address: 1 Middle St
Brighton BN1 1AL, UK
Phone: +44 1273 778191

#261
Tom's Bar
Category: Bar
Average price: Expensive
Address: 13 Prince Albert Street
Brighton BN1 1HF, UK

#262
Marlborough Hotel
Category: Pub
Average price: Modest
Address: 4 Princes Street
Brighton BN2 1RD, UK
Phone: +44 1273 570028

#263
Queensbury Arms
Category: Pub
Average price: Modest
Address: Queensbury Mews
Brighton BN1 2FE, UK
Phone: +44 1273 328159

#265
Kings Arms Hotel
Category: Pub
Average price: Exclusive
Address: 56 George Street
Brighton BN2 1RJ, UK
Phone: +44 1273 603238

#266
White Horse
Category: Pub
Address: 30-31 Camelford Street
Brighton BN2 1TQ, UK
Phone: +44 1273 603726

#267
Don Quijote
Category: Tapas Bar
Address: 34 George St
Brighton BN3 3YB, UK
Phone: +44 1273 720360

#268
Horatio's Bar
Category: Pub, Karaoke
Average price: Modest
Address: Brighton Pier
Brighton BN2 1TW, UK
Phone: +44 872 148 6075

#269
The Newmarket Arms
Category: Pub
Average price: Inexpensive
Address: 32 Bear Road
Brighton BN2 4DA, UK
Phone: +44 1273 688245

#270
Golf Addiction
Category: Bar
Address: 5 Mermaid Walk
Brighton BN2 5WA, UK
Phone: +44 1273 672198

#271
The Victory Inn
Category: Pub
Average price: Inexpensive
Address: 6 Duke Street
Brighton BN1 1AH, UK
Phone: +44 1273 326555

#272
Yates
Category: Pub, Nightclub, British
Average price: Inexpensive
Address: 59 W Street
Brighton BN1 2RA, UK
Phone: +44 1273 731117

#273
Branch Tavern
Category: Pub
Average price: Exclusive
Address: 52-53 London Road
Brighton BN1 4JD, UK
Phone: +44 1273 606088

#274
Riz Raz
Category: Hookah Bar, African
Average price: Modest
Address: 8 Western Road
Brighton BN3 1AE, UK
Phone: +44 1273 777971

#275
Master Mariner
Category: Pub, British
Average price: Modest
Address: Village Square
Brighton BN2 5WD, UK
Phone: +44 1273 818563

#276
Easy Bar
Category: Pub
Address: 9-10 Cranbourne Street
Brighton BN1 2RD, UK
Phone: +44 1273 710928

#277
The Bat & Ball
Category: Pub
Average price: Inexpensive
Address: 49-51 Ditchling Road
Brighton BN1 4SB, UK
Phone: +44 1273 624984

#278
Faigans
Category: Bar, Italian, British
Address: 50 George Street
Brighton BN3 3YB, UK
Phone: +44 1273 730530

#279
Pond Public House
Category: Pub
Average price: Inexpensive
Address: 49 Gloucester Road
Brighton BN1 4AQ, UK
Phone: +44 1273 621400

#280
The Cow
Category: Pub, British
Average price: Modest
Address: 95/97 Dyke Road
Brighton BN1 3JE, UK
Phone: +44 1273 772370

#281
The Red Rooms
Category: Bar, Music Venues
Address: 8 Queens Road
Brighton BN1 3WA, UK

#282
The Blue Man
Category: African, Moroccan, Jazz & Blues
Average price: Modest
Address: 8 Queens Road
Brighton BN1 3WA, UK
Phone: +44 1273 726003

#283
The Standard
Category: Pub
Address: 77 West Street
Brighton BN1 2RA, UK
Phone: +44 1273 227592

#284
Sky Bar
Category: Bar
Address: 54-55 Meeting House Lane
Brighton BN1 2AA, UK
Phone: +44 1273 207040

#285
Dirty Blonde
Category: Cocktail Bar, American
Address: 75-79 E Street
Brighton BN1 1NF, UK
Phone: +44 1273 727494

#286
Jury's Out
Category: Pub
Average price: Modest
Address: 161 Edward St
Brighton BN2 0JB, UK
Phone: +44 1273 601148

#287
Ali Cats
Category: Music Venues, Jazz & Blues, Pub
Average price: Inexpensive
Address: 80 East Street
Brighton BN1 1NF, UK
Phone: +44 1273 348103

#288
The Hub
Category: Bar
Address: 129 Saint James Street
Brighton BN2 1, UK

#289
Candy Bar
Category: Bar, Nightclub
Address: St James Street
Brighton BN2 1TH, UK
Phone: +44 1273 622424

#290
The Jolly Poacher
Category: Pub
Average price: Modest
Address: 100 Ditching Road
Brighton BN1 4SG, UK
Phone: +44 1273 683967

#291
Cleveland Arms
Category: Pub
Address: 27a Cleveland Road
Brighton BN1 6FF, UK
Phone: +44 1273 077077

#292
Chameleon
Category: Bar, Nightclub
Address: 61a Western Road
Brighton BN3 1JD, UK
Phone: +44 1273 733870

#293
The Wellington
Category: Pub
Address: 12 College Place
Brighton BN2 1HN, UK
Phone: +44 1273 605414

#294
The Rock Inn
Category: Pub
Average price: Modest
Address: 7 Rock Street
Brighton BN2 1NF, UK
Phone: +44 1273 697054

#296
O'Neills Bar
Category: Pub
Average price: Inexpensive
Address: 27 Ship Street
Brighton BN1 1AD, UK
Phone: +44 1273 827621

#297
Kuku Club
Category: Nightclub
Average price: Modest
Address: 10 Pool Valley
Brighton BN1 1NJ, UK
Phone: +44 1273 736618

#298
The Sussex
Category: Pub
Address: 17 St. Catherines Terrace
Brighton BN3 2RH, UK
Phone: +44 1273 732442

#299
Longman
Category: Pub
Address: 2-10 Wilmington Way
Brighton BN1 8JH, UK
Phone: +44 1273 502567

#300
The Easy Bar
Category: Bar
Average price: Modest
Address: 9-10 Cranbourne St
Brighton BN1 2RD, UK
Phone: +44 1273 710928

#301
Long Man Of Wilmington
Category: Pub
Address: Wilmington Way
Brighton BN1 8JH, UK
Phone: +44 1273 502567

#302
Revolution
Category: Nightclub
Address: 77 West St
Brighton BN1 2RA, UK
Phone: +44 1273 806090

#303
Greens Cafe Bar
Category: Pub
Address: 62 West Street
Brighton BN1 2RA, UK
Phone: +44 1273 778579

#304
Regency Pool Club
Category: British, Pool Halls
Address: 63-64 West Street
Brighton BN1 2RA, UK
Phone: +44 1273 821888

#305
Nine Rooms Karaoke
Category: Karaoke
Average price: Modest
Address: 9-12 Middle St
Brighton BN1 1AL, UK
Phone: +44 1273 748263

#306
Stanmer Park Tavern
Category: Pub
Address: 292 Ditchling Road
Brighton BN1 6JG, UK
Phone: +44 1273 552005

#307
The Church
Category: Nightclub
Average price: Expensive
Address: 11 Dyke Road
Brighton BN1 3FE, UK
Phone: +44 1273 747203

#308
The Harlequin
Category: Pub
Average price: Inexpensive
Address: 43 Providence Place
Brighton BN1 4GE, UK
Phone: +44 1273 620630

#309
Berlin Bar
Category: Wine Bar
Address: 3-5 Ship St
Brighton BN1 1AD, UK
Phone: +44 1273 206580

#310
The Deep Bar
Category: Lounge
Address: West Street
Brighton BN1 2RE, UK

#311
Brunswick Beer Festival
Category: Bar
Address: Old market
Brighton BN1 2NR, UK

#312
Bennetts
Category: Wine Bar
Address: 32 Egremont Place
Brighton BN2 0GA, UK
Phone: +44 1273 674456

#313
The Hollingbury
Category: Pub
Address: 1 Roedale Road
Brighton BN1 7GB, UK
Phone: +44 1273 555858

#314
Bevendean Hotel
Category: Pub
Average price: Modest
Address: 50 Hillside
Brighton BN2 4TF, UK
Phone: +44 1273 607246

#315
Shakespeares Head
Category: Pub, British
Average price: Modest
Address: 1 Chatham Place
Brighton BN1 3TP, UK
Phone: +44 1273 329444

#316
The Green Muse
Category: Bar
Address: 11 York Place
Brighton BN1, UK

#317
Above The Hobgoblin Venue
Category: DJs, Music Venues
Average price: Inexpensive
Address: 31 York Street
Brighton BN1 4GU, UK
Phone: +44 7891 965045

#318
Sticky Mikes Frog Bar
Category: Bar
Average price: Modest
Address: 9-12 Middle Street
Brighton BN1 1AL, UK
Phone: +44 1273 749465

#319
The Brewery Tap
Category: Wine Bar, Pub
Address: 103 North Street
Brighton BN1, UK
Phone: +44 1273 933484

#320
Bar 76 Club
Category: Nightclub, Cocktail Bar
Average price: Modest
Address: 76 Preston Street
Brighton BN1 2HG, UK
Phone: +44 7761 166300

#321
The Honeyclub
Category: Nightclub
Average price: Modest
Address: 214 Kings Road Arches
Brighton BN1 1NB, UK
Phone: +44 7000 446639

#322
The Verdict
Category: Jazz & Blues
Average price: Inexpensive
Address: 159 Edward Street
Brighton BN2 0JB, UK
Phone: +44 1273 674847

#323
Rendezvous Fun Casino
Category: Adult Entertainment
Address: Kings Rd
Brighton BN1 2FW, UK
Phone: +44 7511 866448

#324
Project56
Category: Gay Bar
Address: 56 George Street
Brighton BN2 1RJ, UK
Phone: +44 1273 623399

#325
Castle Snooker Club
Category: Pool Halls
Address: 22-23 Castle Street
Brighton BN1 2HD, UK
Phone: +44 1273 382246

#326
Craft Beer Company
Category: Pub
Address: 22-23 Upper N Street
Brighton BN1 3FG, UK

#327
Riki Tik
Category: Pub
Address: 18 Cranbourne Street
Brighton BN1 2RD, UK
Phone: +44 1273 683844

#328
Bus Bar Company
Category: Bar
Average price: Modest
Address: 6 Kensington Gardens
Brighton BN1 4AL, UK
Phone: +44 1273 565916

#329
Ten Green Bottles
The Wine Shop & Tasting Room
Category: Bar, Beer, Wine & Spirits
Address: 9 Jubilee Street
Brighton BN1, UK
Phone: +44 1273 567176

#330
The Late Lounge
Category: Cocktail Bar
Address: 14 Ship Street
Brighton BA1 1AD, UK
Phone: +44 1273 728221

#331
Rileys Sports Bar Brighton
Category: Pool Halls, Sports Bar
Address: Oxford Place
Brighton BN1 4JH, UK
Phone: +44 1273 604375

#332
Shooshh
Category: Nightclub
Address: 214 Kings Road Arches
Brighton BN1 1NB, UK
Phone: +44 1273 202807

#333
Beachigogo Bar
Category: Lounge
Address: 211 Kings Road
Brighton BN1 1NB, UK
Phone: +44 1273 202807

#334
Poison Ivy
Category: Bar
Address: 129 St James Street
Brighton BN2 1, UK

#335
PsychoSocial
Category: Events & Venues
Average price: Modest
Address: 1-2 Morley Street
Brighton BN2 9RA, UK

#337
J W Lennons
Category: Pub
Average price: Inexpensive
Address: 116-117 Edward Street
Brighton BN2 0JL, UK
Phone: +44 1273 687515

#338
Fat Poppadaddys
Category: DJs
Address: 10-11 Lewes Road
Brighton BN2 3HP, UK
Phone: +44 1273 607172

#339
The Haunt
Category: Nightclub
Average price: Modest
Address: 10 Pool Valley Coach Station
Brighton BN1 1NJ, UK

#340
The Cleveland
Category: Pub
Average price: Expensive
Address: 27 Cleveland Road
Brighton BN1 6FF, UK
Phone: +44 1273 502396

#341
The Prince Arthur Pub
Category: Pub
Address: Desn Street
Brighton BN1 3EG, UK

#343
The Hanover Canteen
Category: Pub
Address: Elm Grove
Brighton BN2 3DD, UK

#346
Brighton Belles
Category: Massage, Adult Entertainment
Address: 1 Montpelier Road
Brighton BN1 2LQ, UK
Phone: +44 1273 720696

#348
Woo Woo
Category: Cocktail Bar
Address: 56 King's Rd
Brighton BN1 1NA, UK

#349
2 One One
Category: Bar
Address: 211 Kings Road Arches
Brighton BN1 1NB, UK
Phone: +44 1273 324884

#350
The Paris House
Category: Wine Bar
Address: 21 Western Road
Brighton BN3, UK
Phone: +44 7587 784802

#351
Bohemia Grand Cafe & Late Lounge
Category: Cocktail Bar
Address: Meeting House Lane
Brighton BN1 1HB, UK
Phone: +44 1273 777770

#352
KooKlub
Category: Nightclub, Social Club
Address: 10 Pool Valley
Brighton BN1 1NJ, UK
Phone: +44 1723 888000

#353
Bar56
Category: Bar
Address: 56 George Street
Brighton BN2 1RJ, UK

#354
Neighborhood
Category: Bar
Address: 18 Madeira Place
Brighton BN2 1TN, UK

#355
Waves Cafe Bar
Category: Bar
Address: 6-8 Madeira Drive
Brighton BN2 1PS, UK
Phone: +44 1273 620449

#356
The Wellington
Category: Pub
Address: 53 Elm Grove
Brighton BN2 3ET, UK
Phone: +44 1273 603675

#357
Polar Bar East
Category: Pub
Address: 8 St Georges Road
Brighton BN2 1EB, UK
Phone: +44 1273 683334

#358
St George's Inn
Category: Pub
Average price: Modest
Address: 33 Sudeley Street
Brighton BN2 1HE, UK
Phone: +44 1273 694265

#359
Koba
Category: Bar
Average price: Expensive
Address: 135 Western Road
Brighton BN1 2LA, UK
Phone: +44 1273 720059

#360
Woo Woo
Category: Bar
Address: West Street
Brighton BN1 2RE, UK
Phone: +44 845 296 8590

#361
The Couch
Category: Pub
Address: 82 Dyke Road
Brighton BN1 3JD, UK
Phone: +44 1273 721285

#362
Zoot Street
Category: Pub
Address: 8 Queens Road
Brighton BN1 3WA, UK
Phone: +44 1273 737770

#363
Polar Central
Category: Pub
Address: 11-12 Queens Road
Brighton BN1 3WA, UK
Phone: +44 1273 325793

#364
Bell View
Category: Pub
Address: 67 Buckingham Place
Brighton BN1 3PQ, UK
Phone: +44 1273 748849

#365
Belle Vue Catering
Category: Pub
Address: 67 Buckingham Place
Brighton BN1 3PQ, UK
Phone: +44 1273 730219

#366
Brighton Artists Gallery
Category: Bar
Address: 108a Dyke Road
Brighton BN1 3TE, UK
Phone: +44 1273 711016

#367
Bon Appetite
Category: Pub
Address: 48 West Street
Brighton BN1 2RA, UK
Phone: +44 1273 732832

#368
Nellie Peck Public House
Category: Pub
Address: 57 West Street
Brighton BN1 2RA, UK
Phone: +44 1273 382193

#369
Rarekind Art Gallery
Category: Pub
Address: 102 North Road
Brighton BN1 1YE, UK
Phone: +44 1273 818170

#370
Breeze
Category: Bar
Address: 98 Trafalgar Street
Brighton BN1 4ER, UK
Phone: +44 1273 693377

#371
Stanley International Casino
Category: Social Club, Casino
Address: 6-8 Preston Street
Brighton BN1 2HN, UK
Phone: +44 1273 725101

#372
BYOC Brighton
Category: Cocktail Bar
Address: 41 Meeting House Lane
Brighton BN1 1HB, UK
Phone: +44 1273 823383

#373
The Spotted Dog
Category: Pub
Address: 13 Middle Street
Brighton BN1 1AL, UK
Phone: +44 1273 710444

#374
Pasha's Studio
Category: Nightclub
Address: 44 Providence Street
Brighton BN1, UK

#375
Oriental The Public House Mobile
Category: Pub
Address: 5-6 Montpelier Road
Brighton BN1 2LQ, UK
Phone: +44 7071 200865

#376
Sumo
Category: Bar
Address: 9-12 Middle Street
Brighton BN1 1AL, UK
Phone: +44 1273 749465

#377
Wahoo Brighton
Category: Bar
Address: 77 W Street
Brighton BN1 2RA, UK
Phone: +44 1273 719364

#378
Polar Bar
Category: Pub
Address: 113-114 Western Road
Brighton BN1 2AB, UK
Phone: +44 1273 733245

#379
10 Below
Category: Jazz & Blues
Address: 10 Ship Street
Brighton BN1 1AD, UK
Phone: +44 1273 328439

#380
Mission Control Club
Category: Pub
Address: 135 Kings Road
Brighton BN1 2HX, UK
Phone: +44 1273 728999

#381
Mission Control Club
Category: Pub
Address: 135 Kings Road
Brighton BN1 2HX, UK
Phone: +44 1273 728999

#382
Bystander Shisha Lounge
Category: Lounge, Music Venues
Address: 35 London Road
Brighton BN1 4JB, UK
Phone: +44 7500 696996

#383
Top Totty Club
Category: Adult Entertainment
Address: 75 Grand Parade
Brighton BN2 9JA, UK
Phone: +44 1273 689503

#384
Pedestrian Arms
Category: Pub
Address: Foundry Street
Brighton BN1 4AT, UK
Phone: +44 1273 697014

#385
The Honey Club
Category: Nightclub
Address: 214 Kings Rd Arches
Brighton BN1 1NB, UK
Phone: +44 1273 202807

#386
Cube Bar
Category: Cocktail Bar
Address: 5-5a Castle Square
Brighton BN1 1EG, UK
Phone: +44 1273 777200

#387
The Druids Arms
Category: Pub
Address: 79 Baker Street
Brighton BN1, UK
Phone: +44 1273 680596

#388
Red Seven Leisure
Category: Pub
Address: Kensington Street
Brighton BN1 4AJ, UK
Phone: +44 1273 872200

#389
Mot Shop
Category: Adult Entertainment
Address: North Street
Brighton BN1 1RH, UK
Phone: +44 1273 416362

#390
Project
Category: Nightclub, Music Venues
Address: West Street
Brighton BN1 1AZ, UK
Phone: +44 1273 321628

#391
Zanzibar
Category: Bar
Address: 129 St James's Street
Brighton BN2 1TH, UK
Phone: +44 1273 622100

#392
Spread Eagle
Category: Pub
Address: 20 Albion Hill
Brighton BN2 9NP, UK
Phone: +44 1273 686049

#393
Pleisure Public House Management
Category: Pub
Address: 11 Marlborough Place
Brighton BN1 1UB, UK
Phone: +44 1273 628400

#394
Golden Lion
Category: Pub
Address: 7-9 Manchester Street
Brighton BN2 1TF, UK
Phone: +44 1273 601450

#395
20:20 Magazine
Category: Bar
Address: Middle Street
Brighton BN1 1AL, UK
Phone: +44 1273 382020

#396
Bar Revenge
Category: Bar
Address: 5-7 Marine Parade
Brighton BN2 1TA, UK
Phone: +44 1273 608133

#397
The Greys
Category: Pub
Address: 105 Southover Street
Brighton BN2 9UA, UK
Phone: +44 1273 680734

#398
Neighbourhood
Category: Bar
Address: 101 St James Street
Brighton BN2 1TP, UK
Phone: +44 1273 673891

#399
Devonshire Arms
Category: Pub
Address: 52 Carlton Hill
Brighton BN2 0DA, UK
Phone: +44 1273 682376

#400
Montreal Arms
Category: Pub
Address: 62 Albion Hill
Brighton BN2 9NX, UK
Phone: +44 1273 607790

#401
Black & White Love Link
Category: Pub
Address: 44 Washington Street
Brighton BN2 9SR, UK
Phone: +44 1273 624903

#402
Zelgrain
Category: Pub
Address: 146 Springfield Road
Brighton BN1 6BZ, UK
Phone: +44 1273 550000

#403
Brighton Unity
Category: Pub
Address: 131 Islingword Road
Brighton BN2 9SH, UK
Phone: +44 1273 676688

#404
No Name Bar
Category: Pub
Address: 81-82 ST. James's Street
Brighton BN2 1PA, UK
Phone: +44 1273 693216

#405
Lo Lounge
Category: Lounge
Address: Kings Road
Brighton BN1 2FU, UK
Phone: +44 1273 720710

#406
Zap Club
Category: Nightclub
Address: 189-192 Kings Road Arches
Brighton BN1 1NB, UK
Phone: +44 1273 202407

#407
The New Vic
Category: Pub
Address: 31a Richmond Road
Brighton BN2 3RL, UK
Phone: +44 1273 675906

#408
The Victoria
Category: Pub
Address: 31a Richmond Road
Brighton BN2 3RL, UK

#409
Jolly Brewer
Category: Pub
Address: 176 Ditchling Road
Brighton BN1 6JA, UK
Phone: +44 1273 500295

#410
Black Horse
Category: Pub
Address: 16 Montague Place
Brighton BN2 1JE, UK
Phone: +44 1273 698195

#411
Ooosh! Tours
Category: Music Venues
Address: Enterprise Point
Brighton BN2 3LH, UK
Phone: +44 1273 767155

#412
Freshfield Inn
Category: Pub
Address: 230 Freshfield Road
Brighton BN2 9YD, UK
Phone: +44 1273 604829

#413
Leisure Time Consultants
Category: Pub
Address: 213 Preston Road
Brighton BN1 6SA, UK
Phone: +44 1273 500349

#414
Station Hotel
Category: Pub
Address: 1 Hampstead Road
Brighton BN1 5NG, UK
Phone: +44 1273 501318

#415
The Black Dove
Category: Pub
Average price: Modest
Address: 74 St James St
Brighton BN2 1PA, UK
Phone: +44 1273 671119

#416
The Bohemian Lounge
Category: Lounge, British
Address: 58 St Georges Road
Brighton BN2 1EF, UK

#417
Sudeley Arms
Category: Pub
Address: Sudeley Street
Brighton BN2 1HE, UK
Phone: +44 1273 682991

#418
Newbush
Category: Pub
Address: 1 Arundel Road
Brighton BN2 5TE, UK
Phone: +44 1273 687145

#419
Chez Nous
Category: Pub
Address: 1 Arundel Road
Brighton BN2 5TE, UK
Phone: +44 1273 682159

#420
A & M Club Lighting
Category: Nightclub
Address: 7 Cliff Road
Brighton BN2 5RD, UK
Phone: +44 1273 623091

#421
Rock and Roller
Category: Bar
Address: 95 Western Road
Brighton BN1 2LB, UK
Phone: +44 1273 710014

#422
Hanrahans
Category: Pub
Address: Village Square
Brighton BN2 5WD, UK
Phone: +44 1273 819800

#423
Ancient Mariner
Category: Pub
Average price: Modest
Address: 59 Rutland Road
Hove BN3 5FE, UK
Phone: +44 1273 748595

#424
The Brunswick
Category: Pub
Average price: Modest
Address: 3 Holland Road
Hove BN3 1JF, UK
Phone: +44 1273 733984

#425
The Hove Kitchen
Category: Pub, British, European
Average price: Modest
Address: 102-105 Western Road
Hove BN3 1FA, UK
Phone: +44 1273 725495

#426
Hove Place
Category: Pub
Average price: Modest
Address: 37 First Avenue
Hove BN3 2FH, UK
Phone: +44 1273 738266

#427
Royal Sovereign
Category: Pub
Average price: Modest
Address: 66 Preston Street
Brighton BN1 2HE, UK
Phone: +44 1273 323289

#428
Sussex Cricketer
Category: Pub
Average price: Modest
Address: Eaton Road
Hove BN3 3AF, UK
Phone: +44 1273 771645

#429
The Bell
Category: Pub, British
Average price: Modest
Address: 15-17 Belfast Street
Hove BN3 3YS, UK
Phone: +44 1273 770773

#430
Westbourne The Public House
Category: Pub
Average price: Modest
Address: 90 Portland Road
Hove BN3 5DN, UK
Phone: +44 1273 823633

#431
Bali Brasserie
Category: Bar
Average price: Modest
Address: Kingsway Court
Hove BN3 2LP, UK
Phone: +44 1273 323810

#432
Latino Restaurant
Category: Cocktail Bar, Tapas Bar
Average price: Modest
Address: 36 Church Road
Hove BN3 2FN, UK
Phone: +44 1273 770355

#433
Coopers Cask
Category: Pub
Average price: Modest
Address: 3 Farm Road
Hove BN3 1FB, UK
Phone: +44 1273 736945

#434
9 Bar
Category: Bar
Average price: Modest
Address: 120 Church Road
Hove BN3 2PG, UK

#435
Greenhouse Effect
Category: Pub, Music Venues
Average price: Modest
Address: 63 Church Road
Hove BN3 2BD, UK
Phone: +44 1273 204783

#436
Exchange Inn
Category: Pub
Address: 8 Goldstone Street
Hove BN3 3RL, UK
Phone: +44 1273 821677

#437
The Seafield
Category: Pub
Average price: Modest
Address: 150 Church Road
Hove BN3 2DL, UK
Phone: +44 1273 735214

#438
Freemasons Tavern
Category: Pub
Average price: Expensive
Address: 39 Western Rd
Hove BN3 1AF, UK
Phone: +44 1273 732043

#439
The Grenadier
Category: Pub
Average price: Inexpensive
Address: 200 Hangleton Road
Hove BN3 7LT, UK
Phone: +44 1273 773852

#440
The Alibi
Category: Pub
Average price: Modest
Address: 22 Victoria Terrace
Hove BN3 2WB, UK
Phone: +44 1273 733983

#441
Neptune Inn
Category: Pub, Music Venues
Average price: Modest
Address: 10 Victoria Terrace
Hove BN3 2WB, UK
Phone: +44 1273 736390

#443
The Nevill of Hove
Category: Pub, Italian, Pizza
Average price: Modest
Address: 214 Nevill Road
Hove BN3 7QQ, UK
Phone: +44 1273 558799

#444
Farm Tavern
Average price: Modest
Address: 13 Farm Road
Hove BN3 1FB, UK
Phone: +44 1273 779886

#445
Modelo Lounge
Category: Lounge
Average price: Modest
Address: 143/145 Church Road
Hove BN3 2AE, UK
Phone: +44 1273 749559

#446
Hove Park Tavern
Average price: Modest
Address: 156 Old Shoreham Road
Hove BN3 7AP, UK
Phone: +44 1273 735622

#447
Evening Star
Category: Pub
Average price: Modest
Address: 55-56 Surrey Street
Brighton and Hove BN1 3PB, UK
Phone: +44 1273 328931

#448
Paris Wine Bar
Category: Wine Bar
Average price: Modest
Address: Church Road Hove BN3, UK
Phone: +44 1273 778013

#449
Slice Sussex Lounge
Average price: Expensive
Address: Church Road
Hove BN3 2EB, UK

#450
The Palmeira Pub
Average price: Modest
Address: 70-71 Cromwell Road
Hove BN3 3ES, UK
Phone: +44 1273 720641

8732629R00084

Printed in Great Britain
by Amazon.co.uk, Ltd.,
Marston Gate.